An Unhistorical Pastoral by John Davidson

John Davidson was born at Barrhead, East Renfrewshire on 11th April 1857.

In 1862 his family moved to Greenock and there he began his education at Highlanders' Academy. Davidson would now spend many years at school and the beginnings of a career in various industries before gaining employment in various schools.

By now literature was a large part of his activities and his first published work was 'Bruce, A Chronicle Play' in 1886. Four other plays quickly followed including the somewhat brilliant pantomimic 'Scaramouch in Naxos' (1889).

With his reputation gradually providing an income he was also able to explore his true medium; Verse. 'In a Music Hall and Other Poems' (1891) together with 'Fleet Street Eclogues' (1893) were ample proof that he possessed a quite rare, genuine and distinctive poetic gift.

Davidson now turned further and further towards verse. In 1894 he published his most popular volume, 'Ballads and Songs' (1894), and this was followed by a further 'Fleet Street Eclogues' (Second Series) (1896) and by 'New Ballads' (1897) and 'The Last Ballad' (1899).

As the new century dawned Davidson was hard at work on a series of 'Testaments', in which he gave definite expression to his philosophy and were published over a seven year period; 'The Testament of a Vivisector' (1901), 'The Testament of a Man Forbid' (1901), 'The Testament of an Empire Builder' (1902), and 'The Testament of John Davidson' (1908).

However, on 23rd March 1909, with his finances in ruins, the onset of cancer and profound hopelessness and clinical depression he left his house for the last time. His body was only found on September 18th by some local fishermen.

Index of Contents

PERSONS

Alardo, King of Belmarie
Rupert, Alardo's Son
Conrad }
Guido }
Felice } Nobles of Belmarie
Bruno }
Torello }
Cinthio, Conrad's Son
Sebastian, a Sea-Captain
Scipio }
Ivy } Rustics
Green }
Celio, a Shepherd
Oberon
Puck
Eulalie
Faustine, Guido's Daughter
Sylvia, a Shepherdess
Onesta, Faustine's Maid
Martha
Titania
A Servant
Fairies
Mayers
Officers

SCENE: Belmarie

In Grenade, at the siege had he be
Of Algesir, and ridden in Belmarie.
Chaucer

AN UNHISTORICAL PASTORAL

Enter **ALARDO** and **CONRAD**.

ALARDO
Safe, sound, on land, and our own land at last.
How long, Conrad, have we been seafarers?

CONRAD
On our disastrous and untimely cruise,
In early spring we merrily embarked.
The trees are greener now than when we sailed,
More softly breathes the air: my lord, I think
About this time last year our ills began,
A honeymoon on ocean's breast gone by.
If I be right—for judgment here is wide,
Since in escapes from icebergs, pirates, perils
Of krakens, quicksands, bloody cannibals,
Storms merciless, and nights of many days—
The married life of those who wed the deep—
All reckoning was lost—hoar, doting time
Repeats the seasons' epic where our ears
Ceased to attend the world-old history,
One year's discordant interlude between.

ALARDO
Well-tempered discord strengthens: if my son
Be but alive and well, life's music glides
In sweeter, richer cadence for this crash.
If in deep ocean's unrobbed tomb, or white
And all unsepulchred, on some bleak coast
His bones lie withering, discord is the theme
Shall din my hearing to eternity.
Do you remember when the envious wave,
Begrudging me so beautiful a boy,
With swift abduction snatched him from the poop,
And swept him from our ken? Mind you his cry
That pierced the howling storm, nor through that shield
Did with a gentler wound transfix our ears?
Saw you his begging hand finger the air,
Then vanish, lastly visible of him?

CONRAD
'Tis deeply graven in my memory.

ALARDO

Ay, as a moving picture's strong impress;
But I was of it—you, a looker-on.
I watched the sneaking waves, the subtle waves,
The sly, the pitiless, the sinewy waves,
Swarm from the cuttle-sea like suckers lithe,
And steal my son to feed its hungry maw.

CONRAD
Indeed, my lord, not to that tongueless grief
Which seized you then, and held you captive long,
Was I prisoner; but I sorrowed both
For your bereavement and my own past lost.

ALARDO
O, you, too, mourn a son!

CONRAD
In infancy
One was reft from me.

ALARDO
Blessed then are you
That know him in Elysium; but I
Have no sweet sunshine gleaming through my tears.
I would not have mine dead e'en to gain heaven;
But life may now be hell: on yon rude shores
Near which we drifted when my son was lost,
They say that human fiends cavern to prey
On hunted ships the tinchel-waves drive in,
Torturing the voyagers for ransom; some
Transporting slaves to burning Afric climes:
Each imaged pang impales my inmost heart.

CONRAD
I said my loss was past, yet, in a sort,
I suffer fresh bereavement every day;
And might with uncurbed fancy harrow up,
As you do yours, my fatherly regard,
But that it boots not to imagine ill,
Where equal chance shows good luck may betide.
My child was lost or stolen, drowned or devoured,
I brood not which; but, in most hopeful mood,
Think soon to see him well; more sluggish thoughts
Would joy to find him any how or where:
And so, piecemeal, my hope is back repulsed
To find content in sure news of his death.

ALARDO

Was it a while ago your son was lost?

CONRAD
Full fifteen years; his age, one half that sum.

ALARDO
Fifteen unsevered years may cool me too,
But grief and I are fresh and all uncloyed;
We drain the utmost sadness that we can.

CONRAD
I bore grief just so passionate a love;
But long before you slight her as I do,
Doubt not that dear joy will seduce your heart:
Your quick-found son will give her to your arms.

ALARDO
How did you lose your son, good Conrad, say?

CONRAD
Indeed I cannot. One soul-sickening night
Nowhere was he discovered. Every haunt
Where curious childhood oft had wandered him
Appeared as wistful for his sight as we;
The mourning echoes called with us his name.
He was my only son—Heaven grant he is!

ALARDO
For you conjecture had an airy stretch,
And hope full complement of anchors strong;
My thoughts are hedged, my only grapnel drags.
Your son was lost from vague remembrance; death
Plucked mine with bony grasp from out my eyes.
Seven years you had a son; and twice that term
Has tamed your sorrow's force: my Rupert's eyes
Had viewed a score of summers: by this count
A century should see me bow to fate;
But I'll be traitor till death vindicate
The all-commanding rule of destiny.

CONRAD
Permit me, sir: such is your present thought.—
Holds your intent to travel in disguise
Thence to our court: to hear what rumour goes
Concerning us; toward you what mind is borne;
To note your subjects' state; with parent's care
To mark what merits praise, what needs reproof,
And understand the country's inmost soul?

ALARDO

I purpose so. Our lives, however short,
And full of toil, have time enough for grief.
Yet stay, my lord: here comes one who shall tell
Which is the pleasantest, most peopled way.
In him, moreover, we will broach the fame
Of our long ventures in a time so brief.—

[Enter **CINTHIO**.

Sea-bred or inland, friend?

CINTHIO

A shepherd, sir.

CONRAD

Where are we, gentle shepherd, by your voice,
And who reigns here?

CINTHIO

In Belmarie, not far
From court, kind stranger, where no courtiers be.
This country's king was lost a year ago:
Yet in a longing hope he is not dead,
The heir-apparent but a regent's power
Decrees to exercise for twice four years.
When that date is expired, if no king come,
The prince intends to fill his father's room.

ALARDO

His father's, say you?
[Aside]
Have I then two sons?
This shepherd dreams.

CINTHIO

Yes; King Alardo, once
Of these broad realms; now, king in heaven, I wot.
Even as earth's bower-maid, Spring, in robes of green
Her naked lady, roused from winter's sleep,
Began to deck, five galleys, new-built all,
With sails of taffeta, and masts of gold,
Pushed from this strand bound on adventures far,
The king, his son, and many a noble knight,
With mariners and fighting-men aboard.
Of this armada not a single ship
Has yet returned to us; nor any spar

Of drifting wreckage tells a woeful tale.
The gallant prince right from his father's eyes
Was hurried in a storm, and, blest by fate,
Snatched from that doom which overwhelmed the rest;
For he was washed ashore and nursed to health
By fisher-folk, whom he has made his friends.
And now he has forsaken courtly state
To live in country freedom for a while;
In Dolorosa's vale he spends the spring.

ALARDO
And what road must we take to reach this place?
[Aside]
I dare not credit him, or else his tale
Is true of some impostor.

CINTHIO
Onward go,
Until that pine-straight pathway radiates
Two branches from its stem, extending still:
That shooting westward winds a mile or two,
And ends in our royal town; the other way,
Toward sunrise, leads to Dolorosa's vale.

ALARDO
Thy kindness, shepherd, merits some reward;
But now our purses are as lank as we.
Rest you assured of worthy recompense
From me in Dolorosa.

[Goes out.

CONRAD
If my old eyes
Deceive me not, I've seen you, sir, before.

CINTHIO
Maybe, sir; though I, witting, ne'er saw you.

CONRAD [Aside]
I'll question him again.—Shepherd, farewell.

[Goes out.

CINTHIO
What lordly wight was this, who, seeming poor,
Would fee a duteous courtesy? He hides
His beams behind a ragged cloud perhaps.

I'll hope to see him in his majesty.

[Enter **SEBASTIAN.**

I came to see you, captain and good friend.
When do you sail?

SEBASTIAN
When we have made an end
Of lading, and have shipped a proper crew;
Perhaps two days hence. How may this touch you?

CINTHIO
Now you impeach my friendship to speak so;
For I would come, and this full well you know,
To clasp my loved Sebastian on the strand,
And drop a tear upon his parting hand,
And fill his sails with breath of heart-felt prayer
To waft him back, outspeeding swiftest air,
Even while his barque degrades into eclipse
Behind the bulging world, as Phoebe slips,
Slackly and slow, over the ocean's rim,
When stars grow bright, and seas and hills grow dim.
But hark, Sebastian, give me careful heed:
Your often-proffered help I sorely need
To aid me in an enterprise of note.

SEBASTIAN
They all are yours—myself, my men, my boat.

CINTHIO
Is there, far distant from the sea's highway,
Unwatched by any eye save that of day—
Or if perfection lights unreasoning eyes,
By gentle beasts, and birds of paradise—
A coral isle, old nature's best-loved child
And latest offspring, nursed by waters wild—
Tamed in that nurture—to rare loveliness,
Whose witchery creates a sweet distress;
An islet Venus might have made her home,
Even as, love-mad, she blossomed from the foam;
Where lovers may beneath a bread-fruit tree
Repose on bedded flowers, by harmony
Of birds and waters lulled to slumber deep;
And by like sounds be roused to waking sleep,
To feed upon their couch's canopy,
And watch what may appear with dreamy eye,
Stirring no limb, save for their gentler ease,

For ministry of love, or what they please?
Methinks you told me once of such a gem,
Descried unsought; or is it my own dream?

SEBASTIAN
In stress of storm I found it: tempest-driven
I took the first port, and I lit on heaven.

CINTHIO
This isle's felicitous, Edenic state
Lacks of perfection, eyes to appreciate;
These are within your office to supply:
What better watchers than Faustine and I?
O, there's the direst need of flying far!
That envious, and most inveterate star
Whose wanton spite is spent in thwarting love
Has chosen us for signal harm; we strove
Against disaster, but are hemmed to this,
Either to fly, or die upon a kiss.

SEBASTIAN
To die upon a kiss?

CINTHIO
Or kiss and die;
For Faustine is a maid of lineage high;
A foundling, and a vulgar shepherd, I.
Her sire's a lordly wight of sternest mould,
Who guides his life and hers by precepts old.
He trains his child in crude simplicity,
That ignorance may foster modesty;
Gives her free scope—in gardens and parterres,
With dowagers and hoary aunts for feres;
So jealous of his name, so mean his measure
Of all feminity, her honour's treasure
He will not trust to any common guard,
But in the night, before her door is barred,
He hides—unchristened trick!—that cloudy dress
Wherein by day her sun-bright nakedness
She mercifully veils from mortal eyes,
To hinder, as he trusts, all enterprise,
Such as we purpose with the treacherous aid
Of that twice-suborned spy, my lady's maid;
Which, with your help, we've sworn to amplify,
Or on an everlasting kiss to die.

SEBASTIAN
Yet wherefore fly to such a far-off isle?

Unbroken time to love, and nature's smile,
With safety unmolested, you may reach
Upon some neighbouring and less dangerous beach.

CINTHIO
We have solaced our souls with hope of bliss
In that far isle; not there, then paradise:
Being bound for heaven, not storms, not rocks can fray us,
Yea, dreadless death more swiftly would convey us.

SEBASTIAN
Then nothing moves you. Yet, take tent and think:
They need not drown who still stand on the brink;
And let me tell you, if I rightly deem,
These isles are all as fragile as they seem;
Strong as the spider's web, the poor fly's tomb,
Fixed as the rainbow on a crest of foam,
Stable as any luring bright mirage,
Torn into ribbons by the ruthless wind,
Whelmed by the multitudinous waves' wild dash,
Gone like a dream leaving no trace behind.

CINTHIO
If you, my best Sebastian, bear us hence,
We'll prove this doctrine by experience.

SEBASTIAN
Its truth will be expounded by th' event.
Must all things fit that you may sail to-night?

CINTHIO
Not until after midnight, for our flight
Must be with stealth, and cautious management.

SEBASTIAN
Love's gentle goddess prosper your intent!
Two hours past night's dark noon I'll meet you here.

CINTHIO
Farewell till then.

SEBASTIAN
Farewell, and no ill fear.
Of what I said, dissuading, have no care:
Blow high, blow low, we this adventure dare.

[They go out separately.

Enter **ALARDO**, **CONRAD**, and **GUIDO**.

ALARDO
Thus thrice am I the father of one son:
By ordinary geniture and birth;
And by my son's deliverance from death—
Yea, resurrection, for I held him dead;
And now experience within these months
Of our forlorn and shipwrecked wanderings
Has moulded him into a goodly youth,
Refined and brilliant in all inward beauty:
Witness his conduct in the regency:
What prince had nailed such shackles on his power,
Or fixed his bondage for so long a term,
Simply for love of his sire's memory,
Seeing that hope of life there could be none?
This is a certain new-birth; for I feared,
By some hot coltish springs his blood had fetched,
That, boiling high, it might sad trouble brew;
And partly 'twas to coy his restive sprite
I planned that voyage whose conclusion
Had such ill opening, and ends so well.—
Now, heaven forgive my selfishness! Guido,
Go, send out messengers on every coast.
It could not well bechance that we alone
Of all our ship's crew should be now dry-shod:
Yea, and indeed it would be marvellous,
That of five vessels in the self-same track,
Four should be swallowed wholly by the deep.
Bid all the mariners who leave our ports
To pass no ship unspoken they may spy:
We have escaped, so may those who remain:
Till they are landed safe, and not till then
Will I take heart to laugh. Go quickly, sir.

GUIDO
Your grace's mandate needs no issuing,
For penalties have been already paid
By those who disobeyed the prince in this.

ALARDO
He does anticipate our utmost wish.

GUIDO

He is, sire, a right slip of the old tree
We know well whence his rosy graces spring;
Yet, if you should be pricked in finding out
Among these flowers a thorn, be not surprised.

ALARDO
Be not so emblematic, trusty Guido.

GUIDO
I do not, sire, asperse your dead queen's fame
But she was mother to our noble prince;
Now queens are women, and all women are
But women—

ALARDO
'Tis most true; and spades are spades.
Guard well your tongue. Proceed, sir, and be brief.

GUIDO
Pardon, your majesty. You are too quick:
I meant not as your jealousy conceives:
But I will stake my head none of their sex
Are better than their sphere of life requires:
This is their utmost character for good.

ALARDO
Come, we have heard your doctrine many a time:
And, by the way, how does your vestal daughter?
Still in her cloister mewed from eyes profane?
But without more digression, Rupert's fame
Seems by your blazoning a little blurred.
Record me how a bend sinister comes
To blot the fair field of his character.

GUIDO
Being a woman's son, unstable motion,
The loose stone in his virtue's strong rampire,
Threatens a downcome to its battled front;
For he pursues with lewd desire or love—
Both in this case disastrous to a prince—
A maiden of the very humblest strain,
Who, by her beauty's unassisted charms,
Or these and spells of necromantic art,
Has found his weakness: this did I smell out
When his companions' younger noses failed.

ALARDO
That's not so well; but being a man's son

The youthful blood that warmed his father's veins,
Now briskly runs in his. We'll find a bit
To stay its galloping, or suasion soft
To woo it from from such skittish practices.

GUIDO
Please it your highness, now to tell me why
I have been honoured first to taste the joy
Of your long-prayed-for presence in your land,
Rather than to delight at once your son.

ALARDO
I doubted that he was no son of mine,
But some impostor. 'Twas a foolish fear
With hope twin-born by information scant
That there was cause to hope; so, thinking well
That should I rush to this youth unadvised
The fear would like a hated step-child fare,
And passion nurse the longed-for hope alone,
I wisely verified report in you.
Now, use your wits; devise some plan whereby
I may, myself unknown, confer with Rupert.

GUIDO
To-day a custom, ancient, all-observed,
But savouring in my mind of pagan rites,
And unbecoming folk of Christendom,
Is followed by our sheepish villagers,
Who in their day and generation act
What by their ancestors has been performed,
In timely order tumbling in the ditch
Some silly, old, bell-wether age first filled.
to-day our youth are met upon the green
To plot a treason licensed by the time,
Which is, to choose a king and queen of May
To reign to-morrow and each holiday;
To whom, alone, they shall allegiance swear
At every festal season of the year.
There Rupert courts his lovely, well-loved quean,
Who will be crowned, if I guess rightly, queen;
And he, most like, so highly throned by birth,
Will reign their monarch on a seat of earth.
In some disguise conceal your royalty;
Go there; inspect your son, and be as free
As though you wore no mask: every degree
Has access to him in this pageantry.

ALARDO

A very feasible and pleasant plot.
Come, Conrad, comrade us: since by our lot
Comrades we have been for so long a spell
In danger and in woe, it chords right well
That we be still in unison for joy;
You saw me lose, behold me find my boy.

CONRAD
I will, my lord.—Vouchsafe to call to mind
My dead wife's image.

ALARDO
Strange! I am inclined
To think of her full oft within these hours.
I see her now, of many lovely flowers
That graced our youthful court the loveliest;
My sweet, her queen; she, queen of all the rest.
The shepherd whose direction helped us here—
'Tis he recalls your lady's pleasant cheer;
Her voice, her smile, her action, yea, her face,
Stronger, being male, as coy, to suit his place.

CONRAD
He is, indeed, the picture of her youth.
Conviction now lacks nothing of the truth.
He'll be among those playful-treacherous ones,
Where let us haste to find two long-lost sons.

[They go out.

ACT II

SCENE I.—A Room in Martha's House

Enter **EULALIE**.

EULALIE
O little heart of mine, why ache you so?

[Enter **MARTHA**.

MARTHA
Why, child, why! What a state is this! Come! and you to be
Queen of the May! They say Prince Rupert will himself be king.

EULALIE

And that it is that troubles me.

MARTHA
And so it should. Trouble! the highest lady in the land would be so troubled—such a coil would she be in! What kirtle to put on; what flower, or none; she'd spend six hours, I warrant, over her hair. Then her stomacher, her kerchief, and her shoes; her sash, gloves, necklace, each an hour apiece. But what's your trouble, child?

EULALIE
I do not know.

MARTHA
Who was it said just now Prince Rupert troubled her?

EULALIE
I think 'tis he; for when I first was told
That they would have me for their Queen of May
It pleased me as a new gown pleases me.
When Rupert's name was buzzed about for king,
My heart became a hive of busy things
That hum perplexingly: I know them not,
But fear they may have stings: that is my grief.
I cannot tell if it be joy or grief:
To grieve for joy were far more happily sad
Than ever I have been; if joy unmixed,
Then wherefore am I sad? 'Tis melancholy.

MARTHA
Melancholy! Why, child, I would laugh if thou didst not look it. Come; I have that would banish melancholy from a mummy—a new flowered silken dress and ribbons.
I'll dress thee and thou'lt be the loveliest queen
That ever led a dance upon the green.

[Goes out.

EULALIE
The mood which I have christened melancholy
  Is that, I think, which rules a lonely dove:
It wars with maidhood, yet is not unholy:
  I'll rebaptize my melancholy, love:
With dropping tears of virgin purity,
Claiming its soul for spotless chastity.

[Re-enter **MARTHA.**

MARTHA
Hurry! There's not a second, child, to spare;
Indeed it is high time that you were there,

Where all the village waits to make you queen;
And that is what your mother ne'er has been.

[They go out.

SCENE II.—A Garden Before Ruperts House

Enter **FELICE** and **BRUNO**.

BRUNO
Think you the Prince's present humour lasting?

FELICE
Ay, while the relish smacks. This rustication
Is pleasant to him now, a dainty tasting
    Of heather honey; lacking domination
O'er appetite, he'll gorge and surfeit soon
    On country pleasures; sick of nature's sweet,
Of making hay, and gazing on the moon,
    Of hearing kine low, wool-producers bleat,
Cocks crow, crows caw, doves coo, and goslings gabble,
    Of all their junketing and rural sport,
Their ales, mays, harvests, songs and silly babble,
    He'll hasten to the spiced and pickled court.
With all due reverence for mighty Pan,
    Here's one who wishes we might leave to-morrow;
For, by my beard, I'll soon lose all the man
    Hushing my wit, and suckling of that sorrow.

BRUNO
I fear it much; mine is at least asleep:
    Plague on these blowsy girls and brown-faced knaves,
Who rake their brains and set our jests asteep,
    Distilling that which no refining craves,
Concentrating wit's subtle, quaint, quintessence.
    In courtly spheres fat dullards feed fine lights;
But brilliant stars wane swiftly from their crescence
    When doomed to shine among chaotic wights:
Too much damp fuel quells the strongest fire;
    We perish of this plethora of faggots.

FELICE
Respect has wrought a transformation dire:
    We are dead dogs, these creatures are our maggots.
We, air imperial, burn in this gas,
    Which once illumined us, its atmosphere;

I am a beast of burden; you, an ass—
    Slaves, where before our lash was held in fear.
By heaven, our pates the jingling cap befits!
We are the clowns; the country louts, the wits.

BRUNO
Here comes knave Scipio, the Prince's friend,
Stuck like a wild-flower in his love-lock's shade,
Replacing us, poor withered hothouse blooms.
We'll dust his livery with wordy strokes,
And in his own outspoken chaff deride him.

[Enter **SCIPIO**.

FELICE
By Jove, we will!—Come hither,

SCIPIO
Master of wit, lord of a cabbage-bed,
Knight of the cudgel, toady, knave, and clown,
Beseech your mightiness to signify
To us, your humble servants, what's o'clock?

SCIPIO
The clock's hand points now to that very hour
It indexed at the same time yesterday.

FELICE
Sirrah, you lie, because the clock's gone fast.

SCIPIO
Then is it very adverse to your wit.

FELICE
And like to yours, for fast is loose: your wit Is dissipated, drunk; 'tis redolent
Of sour ale and the smoke of tavern ingles.

BRUNO
That is as much as to say it is ailing, and lapped in inkle, in flannel.

SCIPIO
Verily, it is ailing, in sore pangs of travail, having been impregnated by yours; yet will you hate your
offspring. By the cock and the goose!—which is a Grecian oath, and very religious and philosophic—your
wits are mad, stark mad: Democritus, with an acre of hellebore, could not cure them. Gentlemen, I can
prove you the maddest fools out of your own mouths.

BRUNO

Indeed, we are out of our own mouths; for our mouths are within us; but I thought the foolishest and most unruly member had been in the mouth.

FELICE
A fool expose fools! Let the blind lead the blind.

SCIPIO
Nay; set a thief to catch a thief. But shall I advise you of your folly?

BRUNO
Wise men are silent when fools advise.

SCIPIO
Well said; therefore shall I be silent. But no; for that would be for the wise man to follow the fool's advice. Sir, do you seek for anything?

FELICE
I seek for some ripe grain of wisdom in the desert of your brain.

SCIPIO
And how much do you find?

FELICE
Not a stalk.

SCIPIO
He is a fool who seeks that he cannot find; and you a superlative fool to seek in a wilderness, where you are jagged and torn by prickly briars, for what you believe cannot, without the miraculous intervention of Ceres, grow there. Pray, sir, do you seek for anything?

BRUNO
I seek nothing from you.

SCIPIO
What an ass have we here, what a dizzard! He is surely the king of fools who seeks what, being found, will do him no good—namely, nothing: 'tis a folly worthy of that greatest of fools and criminals, old Nick Nemo.

BRUNO
And who may he be?

SCIPIO
Do you seek to know?

BRUNO
Ay.

SCIPIO

Then shall I not tell you.

BRUNO
But you shall, if he were the devil.

SCIPIO
What? Jove help you! Are your wits entirely sublimed, and condensed on the cold sides of the moon like the melancholy bishop's? Now are you—I cannot say how foolish. You would seek to know the devil? O damned fool! who seek to know that which, being found, will do you more harm than good! Out upon you! out upon you!

FELICE
Fellow, do you seek for anything?

SCIPIO
I seek for something, for something in a special way. I mean I do not seek for nothing; nor do I seek that which I cannot find; nor that which, being found, will do me more harm than good. Bruno, 'Twere a gospel to tell us what you do seek for.

SCIPIO
Sirs, I seek to be rid of you; therefore, farewell.

BRUNO
This fellow must be whipt.

FELICE
For being witty? It is very true
His words are fitted for the barest need,
His jests being like himself, but scantly clad,
Of aspect somewhat sour; but this I see
Plain-speaking blunts much sharper wits than we.

BRUNO
I relish not such Spartan-tongued conversers.
The Prince approaches, and in company.

[Enter **RUPERT** and **CINTHIO**.

RUPERT
Ah! do you jest with Scipio? Know him, friends,
    A fellow of a right good stinging wit;
Who will not spare a king for sordid ends,
    But utter all his mind whoe'er he hit.
This shepherd here is of a different sort;
    His present speech will certify you so.—
Cinthio, my mistress is the sole resort,
    And temple of the graces; in her grow
A spring of beauties; and Pandora's dower

By heritage she wears even at this hour.

CINTHIO

I am a lowly youth, and love a maid
    More high than I am low, and oh, so fair!
Her brow might lend the noonday heaven aid
    To shine upon the world with richer glare;
Her eyebrows are twin rainbows; and her eyes
    Peered suns, excelling all that ever shone,
For they illuminate bright red-rose skies
    Of cheeks celestial with a day-long dawn:
Day being ended, scarcely night's blue veils,
    Her fringed eyelids, can enshroud their beams:
Setting or rising radiance never fails
    To mark their absence in the land of dreams.
Sweet cups of perfumed flowers her nostrils be:
    No bees suck there; the odour makes them faint.
Her little chin is bent with dimples three
    Beneath rich fruit her summer blood does paint
With brighter hues than apples on their trees:
    Alas, to me they are forbidden fruit,
Dearer than apples of Hesperides,
    And guarded by as dragonish a brute.
And when her lips do ope they show her teeth
    Like pearly seeds in sliced pomegranate
Breathing an air that balmily agreeth
    With that delicious fruit. O hapless fate,
That orchards up such dainties to be tasted!
Were I their keeper they should not be wasted.

FELICE

Who may this wild hyperbolist be?

SCIPIO

A shepherd who feeds his sheep upon Parnassus. He gets admission to the chimney-corner at the Castalian Inn, being very thick with the Muses, and a minion of mine host, Apollo.

RUPERT

In very sooth the damsel of your heart
    Seems but a copy of my peerless love,
Fashioned by nature's self-admiring art,
    Which yet has failed to equal what it strove,
My goddess' perfect, yet extempore, beauty:
    Whereby this breathing picture, uttered now,
Far short, as you will swear—a lover's duty—
    Of its exalted theme, must languish low
Beneath the high original I praise,
    By two detractions of her copied grace.

Your miniature you finished with her chin;
Look you, where you desisted, I'll begin.
Her neck into her bosom coyly glides;
    It have I never seen, but well I know
Beneath the little billowy bodice hides
    Costlier treasure than the deep can show:
How white it is I cannot realise,
    Because her hands are whiter than the snow
In sunny winters that half-blinds the eyes,
    Vesting the swelling hills in satin so.
Her waist is fitting for so rare a maid;
    Methinks it was not fashioned for an arm;
In whatsoever garment 'tis arrayed
    Too dainty seems it for maternal harm.
The dimples of her cheek and of her chin,
    The blue veins of her brow, her lashes long,
Her faultless arms, her fingers lithe and thin—
    Sometimes a ring appearing them among,
Looks like the little golden coronal
    Round which the petals of the lily cluster:
Her sloping shoulders, and her feet so small,
    That hardly can sufficient courage muster,
Even in the circumlocutory shoe,
    To show themselves in their entirety,
But like a maid's first love-thoughts from the view
    Of her own eyes retire most trepidly.
The limbs above them! Hush, the moonlight pales
    Before their splendour white as sunlight seems.
Her hair! The brightest imagery fails
    To be a proxy for its rippling streams,
Like shimmering wavelets when the sun has set
Where his pale golden glory lingers yet.
When I am with her I need not to think;
    For if she silent sit, or walk, or stand,
My faculties do altogether link
    And chain my eyes upon her by command
Of her magnetic power; or if she speak
    In tones that Mercury might imitate,
Or through her lips a sounding streamlet break
    With rush of sweetest melody, create
Within the coral, pearled grotto of her mouth
    In tones that Philomel could not surpass;
Then does deep hearing cause a summer drouth
    In sense's welling founts, whose waters pass
Into the yawning ocean of my ears,
    Entranced as by the music of the spheres.
Cophetua's bride was humbler than she is;
    Yet is she humblest of the maids I know.

Mage Hymen will transmute girl to princess;
　　My empress love enthroned her long ago.

SCIPIO
I know this wonder.

FELICE
Which the Prince praises?

SCIPIO
Ay. She is indeed a miracle. Her mother is a woman; and there are those who will swear she was once no higher than her grandam's armchair. It is reported that she eats when she is hungry; her liquor, too, most commonly runs down her throat. Rumour says she is of no kin to graymalkin, for without light she cannot see; yet can her eyes pierce a whinstone as woundily as another's: that she can hear in the night, when she has been known to sleep; that she is often stirring in the day; that when she talks, her organ of utterance is her tongue. Those who should know best will certify that her mouth stands across between her nose and her chin. But the oddest thing about her is her gait; for, look you, when she walks, as the old song goes, one leg or t'other will always be first. Lo, our shepherd has gathered the flock of his thoughts: listen, while he shall tell his tale.

CINTHIO
No wealth, power, state, can I bestow upon her,
　　Who dowers me with herself—that trifles all.
I naught possess save unstained youth and honour;
　　But could I purchase it, hers were this ball.
Yea, to my queen the universe I'd give,
　　Fastening her zodiac-girdle with the sun,
Which from its fixture I would swiftly rive
　　By love's unrivalled power. This being done,
The moon I would assail, and, for a brooch,
　　Place it between the fair moons on her breast;
Nor would the ornament on them encroach
　　So pure are they. Nor would I then desist,
But gather all the stars out of their bowers,
　　And with the most magnate a carkanet
String for her neck; with other heavenly flowers
Bead for her richer hair a priceless net;
And ring her fingers, deck her little ears—
So like their homes, the stars would have no fears.

SCIPIO
Well said, shepherd! All the world on our side!
Nothing remains but hell.

CINTHIO
Not even that; for she with piteous tears
Would quench its sulphurous flames.

RUPERT

So it appears
There's naught beneath, on earth, in heaven above,
Remains for me to ornament my love.
And, truly, it needs not; for in her smock
    She would outshine your star-bedizened dear.—
But lo, the mayers to the maypole flock!
    I am resolved to live no more in fear,
But straightway hasten to that company
    Where now my sweetheart is; move her aside;
Tell her I love her heartily and true,
    And ask her to become my darling bride.
Then shall she murmur sweetly, 'I love thee.'
    I'll kiss her then, and gaze into her eyes;
Appoint a near date for our union too,
    And pray for sweet conjunctions in the skies.

[Goes out.

CINTHIO

Permit me, gentlemen, to part from you.

[Goes out.

BRUNO

Willingly, willingly.—A new rival.

FELICE

Then is Scipio cut out too. Come, we'll be friends with him.—Scipio, do you know where the Prince is gone?

SCIPIO

Do I know what kind of beast a lover is? Does he not follow his mistress like a lamb to the slaughter? If she be in the mouth of hell, I warrant you'll find him in the jaws of death, an he be no nearer. The Prince is now upon his way to her.

FELICE

And she?

SCIPIO

Is where he will find her.

FELICE

Which is—?

SCIPIO

Whither I will bring you, if you be so minded; and on the road I will tell you how all the beauteous virginity and lusty bachelory of Dolorosa be even now assembled to choose a May-queen; how thereafter they will go to bed, and sleep till midnight; how they will then journey to the forest accompanied with music and blowing of horns, to gather may-blossoms and birchen boughs, and deck themselves with nosegays and crowns of flowers. What else they may do there I shall also hint at, specifying to what proceedings on the morrow these actions are prelusive.

FELICE
Of all this the light of knowledge has revealed to us somewhat; but concerning Mademoiselle Eulalie, the Prince's sweetheart, we are in Egyptian darkness.

SCIPIO
Behold, her mother is a fisherman's widow, who in her poverty nursed the half-drowned prince, pinching herself and her daughter, who was, if possible, more willing to be starved that the unknown sick gentleman might have dainties. She has no gold but the gold of her hair; and no jewels save her eyes. If beauty be riches, her wealth is incalculable; moreover, it is safely lodged in the bank of health.

FELICE
And the Prince, by legal usury, would increase her beauty if she would permit him.

SCIPIO
Even so. But there is another merchant in terms for this commodity, for such he would make her. He has more bushels of gold than stones of flesh, and more carnality than wisdom. He is as strong as a horse, but a most outrageous braggart, and little better than a coward. He makes great estimation of his personal appearance, and his figure would be passable enough were it not so bent with worshipping his calves. He dresses like a herald or a macer; and grows the eccentricities of fashion into absurdities, lopping such as by their generality have almost become beauties. This great monkey must needs fall in love with my dainty Eulalie; and finding, though he come before her as gaudy as a serpent, that he works no fascination upon her, he has betaken himself to other charms, and hopes to approach her in a shower of gold.

FELICE
But she is no Danae, you would say; and that this would-be Jupiter will find. Now, what do you think? Shall we play some trick upon—what d'ye call him?

SCIPIO

TORELLO
By Jove, I would give something to see him taken down a peg!

BRUNO
We'll peg him. We'll whip him about like a top.

FELICE
Then let us, as we wend along, conclude
Some scheme to harm Torello for his good.

ACT III

Enter **FELICE**, **BRUNO** and **SCIPIO**.

SCIPIO
Yonder he is, puzzling over a paper. Neither of your lordships knows him?

FELICE
No.

SCIPIO
It is no wonder. Since he fell in love he affects a kind of bearish melancholy; secludes himself; feeds his passion on fish, and has gross dreams. It will take some angling to catch him, gudgeon and all as he is.

[Enter **TORELLO**.

Good-day, sir.

TORELLO
Oh!—good-day.

SCIPIO
Here are two gentlemen of the Prince's court, who, their ears being infected with your absolute accomplishments, have been plagued by the unsatisfied desire of your acquaintance.

TORELLO
It is not the first time I have plagued my acquaintance.
Gentlemen, who are you?

FELICE
Felice is my name; my title, lord; my having, handsome; and my expectation, great.

TORELLO
O sir, my name is Torello; my figure is at least as handsome as yours; and my expectation is high and sure.—Your name, sir?

BRUNO
My figure is as God made it; and my expectation ends in salvation.

TORELLO
Mine ends in matrimony.

FELICE
You are he who loves Eulalie.

TORELLO
Here is a copy of verses, a sonnet to her. Will you read it? It will tell you.

FELICE
Are they yours? Did you write them?

TORELLO
I scratched them down this morning.

FELICE [Reading]
> My sweetest sweeting, once again I say
> With no adornment, simply, 'I love you.'
> You ask me for a mint of words mayhap:
> I give you none save these, 'I do love you,'
> In which is melted all my passion's gold.
> Many a white plain have I deluged black
> With overflowing, wordy, rhyming streams;
> But I have found them all too weak, and so
> I simply say and mean, 'I do love you.'

This is excellent.
> You ask me why no tears bedim my eyes:
> I answer, I have drained them dry already.

Better still.
> You ask me why my cheek so rosy is:
> I answer, that I keep my health for you.

O, admirable! This cannot fail to win her.

SCIPIO [Aside]
He may have written it after all.

TORELLO
I will send it to her along with this string of pearls.

SCIPIO
If I might interest myself so far in your lordship's affairs,
I would suggest that, having thus engaged the services of Plutus and
Apollo, you now enlist under your love's flag the potent Hecate.

TORELLO
Ah! I shall consider your counsel.

FELICE
It is good counsel.

TORELLO
Who's this Hecate?

FELICE

She is a sorceress, and has her haunt in the wood. She will tell you how you are to discover that you are to marry Eulalie; and this certain knowledge of futurity, stranded with the verses and the necklace, will form a cable that draws her into your arms.

TORELLO
Into my arms! Let us visit Hecate at once.

FELICE
It is too soon. She will not be approached till the moon is up.

TORELLO
Then come with me, and you shall see Eulalie. But, look you,
I will not make her known to you.
[Aside]
She knows too many men already.

FELICE
It needs not: we will know her by her beauty.

TORELLO
Ay; but you must not speak to her.

FELICE
How if she speak to us?

TORELLO
Then must you be short in your answers, and by no means attempt to gain her favour; I would have her favour no man but me.

FELICE
Fear not us. Courtiers know how to behave, and fishermen's
daughters are excellent wenches.

TORELLO
They are most sweet wenches. Eulalie is a most sweet fisherman's wench.

FELICE
How was he sweet? Did he do business in fresh water only?

TORELLO
What, he? You start from our subject. Come on, come on.

[**BRUNO** and **TORELLO** go out.

FELICE
It will work, I think.

SCIPIO

Assuredly. I know where to get such rig as will pass for a witch's. Bring him along to the place you wot of, and let chance guide our sport.

[They go out.

SCENE II.—An Open Space

Beneath a hawthorn, **EULALIE**, garlanded; near her, **RUPERT**, **FELICE**, **BRUNO**, **TORELLO**, and **SCIPIO**, standing together. **IVY** and **GREEN, ALARDO** and **CONRAD**, dressed like soothsayers, among a crowd of **MAYERS** beside a May-pole.

CINTHIO, apart.

GREEN
Prince Rupert shall our May-lord be.

IVY
Well said!

MAYERS
The prince, the prince!

GREEN [To **EULALIE**]
Fair queen, entreat the prince.

EULALIE
Be you our lord of May, most gracious prince.
I pray you pardon me if I be bold;
Being but a puppet-queen, my subjects' pupil,
I speak as I am urged.

RUPERT
As you are urged?
You are their spokesman, merely?

EULALIE
Queen, they say,
But little more than their spokeswoman, sir.

RUPERT
I mean, you are mouthpiece only for them.

EULALIE
as any other, sir, petitioned you?

RUPERT

You will not understand me. This request
That I should share with you May's flowery throne,
Is, say, the utterance of a hundred hearts,
Well-purged and sweetened to the May-queen's prayer,
And she, the hundred first, breathes only air.

EULALIE
Air, only air, prince, for these hundred hearts:
I speak for them; beseech you, be their king.

RUPERT
The May-queen would not have me for her consort?

EULALIE
O yes, my lord, I would. My own heart's throbs
Are prayers beseeching you to take it all—
To reign, to tyrannise, to enslave, to kill.
My kingdom's conquered now and factious strife
Of modesty and love quelled and atoned
By your dictation; nobles and populace
Crown you, enthrone you, monarch absolute.
I pray you, speak not to me; I would weep.
The blush upon my cheek will hotly burn
Till flooding penitence has quenched its glow.
You are so pertinent an inquisitor,
Your eyes did burn my resolution through,
Your voice did drown me, and I cried for help.—
My lord of May, speak to the people, now.

[She leads him forward and goes out.

TORELLO [Aside]
Now will I offer it to her. Oh! she has tears in her eyes. No; she must be in a merrier mood to think of love.

RUPERT [Aside]
Ay, lord of May, and lord of May again!
May-lord this year, lord of this May for aye;
Lord of this flowery season of love's bloom,
Lord of this flower of love, seasonably blown:
Prince am I—King, maybe, of Belmarie,
May-king, and king of sweet May Eulalie.—
Good friends, we thank you for this title new:
Its fresh addition gives us double power,
With which we join our queen's, two-fold as well,
Strong by your suffrage, by her beauty strong:
And in this combined and quadruple might,
We bid you be as merry as you may.

Let study, commerce, labour, for a time—
In truth, three woes—be counted sins in act;
Shame anger, malice, envy, every ill
Back to the devil with loud-laughing mocks;
Drink hail to liberty in rosy wine;
Happy your faces with continuous smiles,
And spend mirth's overflow in jest and song;
Forsake stone walls; re-live the golden age
Among the trees in sweetness and moonlight.

MAYERS
We will, we will!

RUPERT
Our May-queen gone!

FELICE
She has retired to preserve her beauty.

BRUNO
Ay, sir, to pickle it, to wash it in brine, to weep.

RUPERT
Wept she, indeed?

[They talk apart.

GREEN
Is it not a noble prince?

ALARDO
Truly he seems to be; but by this hue
We may not judge his nature's primal mood;
For princes, in their humours, are chameleons.

IVY
Camellias, sir, are of different colours.
Our prince is of the spotless dye.

ALARDO
Whitewashed—a sepulchre?

IVY
Sir, do you speak well?

ALARDO
Well; I hope I speak as well as other men.

IVY
But do you mean well?

ALARDO
By all means.

GREEN
For he who speaks ill of the prince here, had need to be his bosom-friend, or a cur whom no one would waste a kick on.

ALARDO
The prince must lie warm-covered in your hearts.

IVY
You must be a stranger. Know, that this same Prince Rupert is out of sight and beyond hearing the mightiest monarch in these parts. To the nobles he is a most egregious tyrant; to the commons, a very brother. But yesterday he addressed me by the damnations of knave and fellow: he could not have been more familiar though he had been my own father, who always calls me rascal. His good qualities are as contemptible as another man's sins.

ALARDO
Then, by your showing, worthy villager,
He is a very white crow of a prince.
But, tell me, is he not Alardo's son?

IVY
His son, and successor. Indeed, I may say, he is his father, for he, being without question dead, Rupert is king.

ALARDO
Dead without question! You are positive.
How, if I say I know he is alive?
Think you to gain a sire the prince would choose
To lose so mighty and august a throne?

IVY
Treasonless man! would you dethrone the prince? Ho! lechery and faith! guard our good prince! His life's in danger.

RUPERT
What cry is this?

IVY
Great prince, it might have been a crying matter; but I, thank the gods, have been man enough to stifle it.

RUPERT
So you have turned approver: renegades I never trust; but what have you to say?

IVY
I will prove that this greybeard is the most noteworthy renegade and trusty traitor these times have seen.

RUPERT
Your language is too original for ordinary capacities.—What are you, old man?

ALARDO
A soothsayer.

RUPERT
Is he affiliated in your trade?
His dress betokens that. What have you said
That this clod could construe as treasonable?

ALARDO
I but suggested that your highness' sire
May yet be canopied by yon blue sky,
With no damp mouldering roof, or watery pall
Between him and the tabernacling air;
That you would joy at loss of sovereignty
To clasp Alardo in your arms once more;
Whereon this loyal sirrah bellowed out,
And laid on me officious needless hands.

RUPERT
Ha! those of your profession are not wont
To talk at random even in courtesy.
Approach us nearer; we would speak with you.—
[To **IVY**]
For you, sir—there: we pay your blundering faith.
[To **ALARDO**]
Now, summon to thine aid thy powerfullest sprite;
Or if thy demon be unknown, and speed
All unappealed and unannounced, whether
He fly from heaven or mid-aerial limbo,
Subdue all motion and prostrate thy will,
Yea, let thy soul evacuate, that, void,
Thy genius may usurp its empty fane,
And prophesy with scope and native truth.
To question were to slight thy divination;
Therefore say sooth of all I seek to know.

ALARDO
Two things by thee desired most
Cannot be thine: one must be lost:
One's forfeit is the other's cost.

RUPERT

An oracle. Expound it now, good sage.

ALARDO

Remember one, absent and dear;
Think of another, loved and near;
Their interests clash; their clashing fear.
Before the moon does twice uplight
The dusky countenance of night,
It shall be past, this bosom-fight.

RUPERT

I understand, and half believe, because
On an event so sudden and unlike
As that of King Alardo's re-appearance
Thou stak'st thy fame thus openly. Say more.

ALARDO

No more to-day; I am dispirited:
And never twice 'twixt ruddy morn and morn
Are we with visionary prospect blessed.
Your eyes are on my comrade. Brother, speak.

CONRAD

Nothing to you, Prince Rupert.
There is one
Of lowlier state whom I have news to tell.
He yonder stands and broods with eyes downcast.

RUPERT

Cinthio, hither and hear thy fortune told.

ALARDO

Prince, I have converse for your private ear.

[They talk apart.

CINTHIO

Soothsayers and augurers of old were held
In high repute for dreams and prophecies.
Their star is waning now, their traffic being
Unto a race, better in being busy,
In barren, fallow fancy, how much worse!
Divine you from the stars, old man; or from
Men's shapes, complexions, palms, dreams and the like?
Scan you a mutton's clean-picked shoulder-blade,
Or have you any visionary aid?

CONRAD

I'll tell thee truths about thyself thou know'st not.

CINTHIO

Say on.

CONRAD

Three lustres has this orb in heaven rung,
Swinging around its vast and vaulted bell
Of measured space, striking its own deep knell
From side to side, a huge and pendulous tongue,
Since thou, then five years' journey to thy grave,
    Wast filched most vilely from a lordly home.
Thou shalt not, shepherd, twice Pan's blessing crave,
    Morning and evening on thy flock; nor roam
Upon these hills beneath a twice-risen sun
Before thou find'st a father; he, a son.

CINTHIO

A mutual treasure-trove. But by what sign
May I believe this bare assertion true?

CONRAD

Beneath thy left breast is a crescent mole;
A flame has sealed a kiss upon thy cheek;
A gold chain quaintly wrought hangs round thy neck,
Hidden from every but the second sight.

CINTHIO

By heaven, these things are so! Now, who art thou?

RUPERT

Presumptuous, meddling fool! A plot, a plot!
Confess who bribed thee. Guido 'twas, I warrant.
Cinthio, what says the other?

CINTHIO

He gives me
A noble father at no later date
Than sunset of to-morrow; vouching this
By nominating several private marks
About my body.

RUPERT

So; well-planned, indeed!
Wretched dissemblers, bear these wrinkles hence,
That, being hypocrites, for age is wise,

Shame that which they betoken. Quick, begone!
[To **CINTHIO**]
I'll tell thee more anon.—Stand not agape;
Be off, trudge, trot; away!

[**ALARDO** and **CONRAD** go out.

Good, gentle mayors,
Retire home for a little; lightly sup;
Lightly to bed; at midnight, lightly up,
To welcome May, to banish worldly jars,
And wanton it like twinkling earthly stars,
Outpeering those who then will deftly tread
In joyous, maiden mirth, and all the night
About the pure moon, from whose dark blue bed
Her bower-maids singing sweetly-low aloud
To wake their queen, will, with soft, quaint affright,
Charily cast her coverlet of cloud:
Stars must we all be when shall be displayed
Our May-moon, Eulalie, earth's loveliest maid.

[**MAYERS** go out shouting.

[**FELICE**, **BRUNO**, and **TORELLO** follow.

CINTHIO
Was not this all too hurried, unripe, green?

RUPERT
No; inconsiderate I have not been.
Grant what they prophesied of us should hap,
It proves no science in the heaven's great map,
Nor any other of unearthly mean:
Their boasted foresight is of things past seen,
And their informing spirits, my good lords.
Now, do you scent the plot? In fewest words;
Some certain knowledge of my sire and thine,
Some hint that I would make Eulalia mine,
The haughty stomachs and the fatuous brains
Of my high cabinet, have feared with stains
Upon our line to spring from Eulalie,
Upon their wisdom in permitting me
To have my bent; and so, to change my mind,
Which by their own they fathom, and to bind
Alardo to their penetrating wit,
They taught these two, dismissed, to tempt this hit,
Which, like a boomerang, returns to maim
The flingers, who have made an evil aim.

CINTHIO

It seems to me this argument is lame.

RUPERT

Lame! Had you heard yon dotard tackle me
About the marring of our family tree;
Predicting sad disaster, ruin, death,
O'erhanging state and king, which loosed by breath
Of vows yet to be sworn to Eulalie
Must thunder on us from the cloudy sky;
No fear of wrong would linger in your head,
No doubt would cripple what I now have said.
Or if I blame too widely, sure am I
'Twas Guido sent these rusty prophets here.
This daughter whom he keeps in turret high,
Making by rarity her beauty dear,
In solitude her soul unsullied blows;
And he upon her lofty virtue builds
A loftier castle than his wisdom knows:
He rushes in, disdaining highest guilds
Of Belmarie's nobility, to mate
His daughter with its prince, himself to make
Most potent minister in all the state—
His prince's king, mayhap, for Faustine's sake.
For any thought save this, I have no mind—
My heavenly love is, like a goddess, kind.
I go to seek her. At some other time
Of these predicts we'll reason, or else rhyme.

[Goes out.

CINTHIO

False prophets, or soothsayers, what care I!
For me the thread is spun and cast the die;
The boat is waiting, and the wind is right.
March past, ye steady hours; lead on, midnight.

[Enter **ONESTA**.

Onesta! Hangs this gear where it did?

ONESTA

Alack, alack, it hangs together like a snow-shower in the air.

CINTHIO

Then is it indeed alack. What has unbound our plot?

ONESTA

O, we are all unbound! All undone! twelve o'clock will never, never do.

CINTHIO

How has that hour become refractory which yesterday was most corrigible?

ONESTA

O, she does not lack courage, but her father, he is fractious.

CINTHIO

Her father! what of him?

ONESTA

O, it's all along of him! He goes to bed every night at eleven, as sure as the clock! Upstairs, at every chime creak goes a step, and his stick comes down between, with his other hand on the baluster. And he talks about a new lamp for the landing, as he has done for the last twenty years—not that I remember; but Marjory, who will be seventy to-morrow—that's May-day; and to hear her talking about the May-days when she was young! This very fore-noon she began gabbling, with her toothless old gums, and her beard going wag, wag—

CINTHIO

For God's sake cease thy gabbling and thy wagging, and tell me how Guido has perverted the good-nature of midnight.

ONESTA

La! what a temper you have! I'll tell Faustine how wild a lover she has caught.

CINTHIO

Tell her how wild I am for her dear love, While you stand dallying with our happiness.

ONESTA

Dallying, forsooth, dallying! I'll dally no more between you!

CINTHIO

My fair Onesta, carry this kiss to thy mistress, and keep this one to yourself. Twelve o'clock is not suitable, because?

ONESTA

Because, as I was just beginning to tell you, Guido goes to bed at eleven—I mean, he goes to his chamber then; counts his keys, his money; gets undressed; curses his valet; says his prayers; then a door slams, or a chimney rumbles, or a rat scrapes behind the wainscot, or a loose slate on Signor Guido's own head rattles a noise of its own in his ears, and he yells, 'Thieves! Fire!' and the bell's rung, and the whole household roused up; and every room, every bed, and closet and hole, searched and shook, and hacked and pierced; and out to the garden—

CINTHIO

And is this a nightly performance? But you knew all this before. What prompted you to have us determine our flight for midnight? It must be then, or sooner.

ONESTA
It can't be, it shan't be, either sooner, or later.

CINTHIO
Come, come, remember the crowns.
[Aside]
I believe she's sold herself to the other side.

ONESTA
Perhaps it may be done, perhaps it may: though it's not any more possible now than it was before.

CINTHIO
How are we to manage?

ONESTA
Well, it may be done; for when I remember, there are two old travellers staying with us just now. They take up all Guido's time. Everybody is so busy you would think our house was a bazaar of all the trades; there could not be more ado supposing it was for the interment of a king. About eleven they will be drawing to the hinder end of supper, and every guest busier than his neighbour eating and drinking, and all the servants drudging like millers with a good wind. Come then: my lady will be ready; and you must put the dress in by the window, and wait till she gets it on, for she will have nothing but her night-gown. Then she will come down, and—O lord! I wish I knew nothing of it.

CINTHIO
Can you by no means procure her own apparel?

ONESTA
It is not to be thought of; for her father would know that she could not come at it but by me.

CINTHIO
She will have greater ease in man's attire, And no disguise could better suit our flight. The wood that lies between us and the shore Will hide us till Sebastian's hour has come. Eleven is our hour. Let Faustine know If I come not that death has flown with me; Or that old Time himself at length has gone, And doomsday come to righten every wrong.

[Goes out.

[Enter a **SERVANT**.

ONESTA
Where have you been?

SERVANT
I was sent to invite the prince to sup at our house to-night; and it is good words to ask a man to a good supper. But the prince refused to come, and that is bad words; for it is bad not to choose the good.

ONESTA

Belike the prince has chosen a better supper somewhere else.

SERVANT
Belike he has. Are you going home?

ONESTA
Yes. You go before.

[They go out.

SCENE I.—The Garden of Martha's House

Enter **EULALIE.** While she is speaking, **RUPERT** enters behind.

EULALIE
My tongue must heave my bosom's suffering forth,
Or else into my mouth my prisoned heart
Will leap, and pant its desperate passion there.
Wild love has burst upon me like a storm:
The gathered clouds I knew; not their full freight.
O me! my desperate, foolish, high-pitched love!
Is this my fortitude, my deep-sworn muteness?
Now, blabbing tongue, be silent; for, behold,
How many bright-eyed, heavenly beings peer
From countless windows on my blush, self-called,
And, listening, smile the welkin wide across
At me, plaining anew love's endless tale,
So risible, so old, so stale to them:
Poor, weary stars, no wonder 'tis you wink!
But I have dared to tell myself I love,
And madly to confess to him 'tis he.
O daring, swift such madness to conceive!
O madness, with untimeous haste brought forth!
Nor will I venture on another thing.
The birds are all asleep; so are the winds;
The trees?—Ah, they have tongues and must have ears.
Dear trees, beseech you, tell no tales on me;
And never, when the wind would have you sing
Chant this sweet name which I will utter now,
Hereafter dreaming nevermore of Rupert.
Nay, gentle trees, you may sigh low his name,
And make all winds in love with that sole word,
Till northern pine-trees rustle it, and know,
As well as southern palmy groves, to teach

Their feathered choirs the syllables I love:
Ye streams and rivers, thou deep-swelling sea,
Confine your far-ranged voices to that theme:
Ye crystal ringing spheres the echo catch.

RUPERT [Aside]
Now will I kiss her. No, her melting heart
Exhales in words still. Hush, my heart; she speaks.

EULALIE
These are sweet thoughts; as sweet as foolish they.
Though all the myriad voices of the world
Should thunder Rupert far up into space
Until the moon swerved from her circling path
Distracted by the noise, I, bidding now,
'Twould only waste breath and the spheres endanger,
For it could not avail to make him love me.
I wish that it were ever night, and I
Could hold converse with it concerning Rupert.
Poor dreamer! have I not appointed this
For my fantastic, final love-discourse!

RUPERT
And of true love's lasting communion first.

EULALIE
O, let me go!—My lord, I did not mean
My treason to be heard by any one.
To princes people are all hypocrites;
And sovereigns all believe that they profess
Which from a true desire to please is said:
This is what should be truth—I love you not.

RUPERT
Treason most capital! Lov'st thou not me,
Thy prince, thy king? For this I rede thy doom:
Full twenty thousand kisses shalt thou pay,
And twenty thousand kisses after these,
As many more when these have been discharged,
To be due always, every hour of the day,
To him 'gainst whom thou hast conspired to cheat
Of what thou longest, burnest to bestow.
O, perjured felon, to thyself and me,
Begin fulfilment of this penalty.

EULALIE
Are you so peremptory? Am I lost?
Think that you heard no syllable of mine,

For you did apprehend my thoughts, as they
Transgressed my own decrees, into night's ear,
And must not prosecute their wantonness,
Since I, their mistress, have forgot their crimes—
This, recent, and that past, done to your face—
Not knowing if I have forgiven them.
I pray you, sir, forget them too—I pray you.

RUPERT
Ah, thou dost fear the honour of my love!
I will forget. Therefore, fair Eulalie,
Most worshipful and low-adored goddess,
I love thee more than any tongue can tell,
And more than all the world beside can love;
More lovingly, more truly, I love thee
Than any lover that has ever loved.
Dost thou love me, and wilt thou marry me?

EULALIE
I love thee with a love not to be shouted:
It is as huge and glowing as the sun,
And it will burn when that clear lamp is out:
Thou art its infinite vitality:
It is as spacious as the element,
And thou art heaven and earth, and all between.
Marry thee, Rupert, Prince of Belmarie?
I know I dream. Ah me, when I shall wake!

RUPERT
I know I dream not: lips so sensible,
So warm as thine, no dreamy spectre bears.

EULALIE
In sleep love's ecstacy's omnipotent.
So sweet a dream as this were best soon done,
That lasting memories may less deplore.
Good-night, fair vision: heaven languishes for thee;
Thine absence has bedimmed its radiance.

RUPERT
I am thy true love, and thou dost not dream:
'Tis not thy wraith, but thee thyself I clasp.

EULALIE
O, art thou flesh and blood? Dear love, good night.
I'll not believe I have no filtre quaffed,
And am not wandering in some blissful land,
Where midnight and pale moonshine ever reign,

And lover's wishes are made true events,
Unless I light my lamp in my own room
And see my bed unruffled. Good-night, love.—
Pluck me a rose that I may surely know
It is no waking vision I have seen,
If I should find I have not been asleep.
Exquisite dream, come to the door with me.

[They go out.

RUPERT [Re-entering]
O, I am new-born, fit for highest deeds!
Now, could I, like old Atlas, bear the world
With all its cares upon my shoulders twain,
And say 'twas light, if but my finger-tips
Rested upon my sweetheart's lily hand.
I'll to the woods till Eulalie has found
Our love is true and sweeter than a dream.

[Goes out.

SCENE II.—An Eminence in a Wood

Enter **FELICE**, **BRUNO** and **TORELLO**.

TORELLO
May this sorceress be approached safely?

FELICE
O, she'll not bite.

BRUNO
She'll only give you a bit of her mind.

TORELLO
I may chance to give her a bit of mine if she be not civil.

BRUNO
A bit is good for a jade.

TORELLO
By Jupiter, she'd best play me no jade's tricks. Shall we on?

FELICE
Yes; over this knoll.

[Enter **RUPERT.** He does not observe the others.

RUPERT
I see thee, moon, in thy high heavenly garden;
Thou walkest like a maid among her flowers.
But thou art not more beautiful, I ween,
Than she who gave herself to me to-night
Within an earthly garden.—Perhaps she sleeps.
O elves unseen, and far away from me,
Who dance upon the shore; and fairies, who
Enamel green hill-tops with little rings
Where merry balls are held; and all ye sylphs
Inhabiting dark shades and rustling bowers;
Ye naiads who make silver streams your haunts,
And ye aerial ones who chant high songs
Against the twinkling of the lyric stars:
From distant vales and hills of Greece o'erskip
The intervening countries at a bound
Ye ancient deities—if ye be dead,
Let your ghosts rise from flowery sepulchres,
Or coral tombs beneath the blue Aegean:
Ye little dwarfs and legendary people
In forest black, or by the oft-sung Rhine,
Or in the moonless caves of furthest Thule,
Desert your homes to-night: and all together,
Quaint, lovely, beauteous, delicate, and droll,
Troop to my lady's chamber: be her dream.

[Goes out.

TORELLO
Dragons and scorpions, hippogriffs and asps,
Hobgoblins, and the ghosts of murderers,
And fiery devils in a fierce nightmare
Confound this fellow's folly!

FELICE
Are you mad?

TORELLO
Tell not me! Eulalie loves him. It was her he spoke of.

FELICE
Are you mad? What he and she?
[To **BRUNO**]
Follow this foolery with me. We'll persuade him he has not seen Rupert.—What trance were you
in for a minute's space, and, being roused, why do you tear your beard? What vision have you seen?

TORELLO
Would you befool me? I'll after, and defy him.

FELICE
Defy whom?

TORELLO
The prince.

FELICE
Of the powers of the air?

TORELLO
Prince Rupert.

FELICE
Ha! be careful what you do. But he is within doors just now.

TORELLO
Within doors! I hear his tread.

FELICE
What! Is he coming hither?

TORELLO
No; he is going hence.

FELICE
Let me understand you.

TORELLO
Understand that I am not deaf; and, having heard Rupert, leaning against that tree, talk like a happy lover, I perceive at once that he must have been accepted by Eulalie: therefore I will challenge him.

FELICE
Love has turned his brain. Did you see Rupert, Bruno?

BRUNO
Not since he left us.

FELICE
Nor I.

TORELLO
Did you not see him put his shoulder against that tree, fold his arms, gaze at the moon, and talk; then with a skip and a hop caper away as merrily as a schoolboy from school?

FELICE

By Luna's horns, but this is wonderful! It cannot be—yet have you not a powerful imagination?

TORELLO

I scarce know; I think so: I am strong.

FELICE

So strong you do not know your own strength?

TORELLO

I have never found its match.

FELICE

That explains this rhapsody, then. Your imagination has been slumbering. Love comes and rouses it, and, like all newly awakened gifts, it attempts great things. Being in keeping with your other qualities, of immeasurable strength, it creates a concretion: you have here, without doubt, suddenly and potently summoned up this apparition of Rupert, its spoken nonsense and ridiculous gait. It must be so. Sir, your imagination is godlike.

BRUNO

Torello, my imagination cannot form a metaphor to express the admiration, the reverence, your genius inspires in me. Many a poetical dreamer would thank God on his knees for a tithe of your gift.

TORELLO

Did you not see the prince?

FELICE

With that solemn face! Ha, ha! You carry the jest; but you cannot create a vision for our eyes.

BRUNO

Come; deride us no longer. Confess you have befooled us.

TORELLO

We are all befooled, I think. This sorceress is charming us.

FELICE

Love, I say, stirred your imagination to plant this jealous fancy against that ash, and gave it language chiming with your fear, and hath almost persuaded you of its reality. To the witch, and be satisfied.

TORELLO

Ay, let us to the witch. She may have sent this vision to spur me on. What shall I say to her?—I would swear I saw Rupert.

FELICE

We'll teach you what to say as we go.

[They go out.

SCENE III.—Another Part of the Wood

Enter on one side **GREEN** and **IVY**, tipsy; on the other **CELIO** and **SYLVIA**, singing.

Song.
    O, the day is loud and busy!
        Every blush the sun discovers.
    Loud and busy, bright and bold,
        Day was never loved of lovers.
    Night for nightingales and moonlight!
        Many a blush night's mantle covers.
    Night for kissing, night for loving,
        Night for us, for we are lovers!

IVY
What singers be these?

GREEN
A shepherd and his lass.

IVY
I know a better song than that. It goes this way:
[Sings]
Night and day let us be merry,
And set not by the world a cherry;
For dry bread chokes—
That's not right. I forget it. I could make a better song than either myself; by my soul, I could! None of your sheepish love-songs, but a song to make the stars dance quicker, and the moon multiply itself a score of times. You have only made two moons.

CELIO
We did not aim at putting the moon beside herself.

IVY
I could make a song about the moon. Sir, I have read about the moon. Her name—hic!—her name is—hic!—

CELIO
Hecate.

IVY
Give a man time to speak his mind. Her name is Hecate, although you say it. I know about the moon: Hecate is the moon—Hecate.

SYLVIA
O, come away!

CELIO

Make your song, my friend, and show it to me to-morrow.

IVY

I will, sir; I will.

CELIO

Good-night.

[**CELIO** and **SYLVIA** go out.

IVY

The song is coming, Green; it's coming. 'By the light of Hecate's lamp'—lamp, lamp—what rhymes with lamp?—Come to some more delusive, poetic spot.—'By the light of Hecate's lamp'—lamp?—Come.—What the devil rhymes with lamp!—Come.

[**IVY** and **GREEN** go out.

[Enter hurriedly **CINTHIO**, and **FAUSTINE** dressed as a shepherd-boy.

FAUSTINE

O Cinthio, hearken! We are lost. Alas!

CINTHIO

Fear not, my love: all danger we shall pass.

[They go out.

SCENE IV.—A Room in Martha's House

Enter **MARTHA**.

MARTHA

Gone with the Prince! I knew 'twould come at last.
Well, I shall be a lonely woman soon.
To think how many a mother envies me
My lovely daughter for her loveliness,
And that she has enchanted our good prince,
And all the happiness in store for me,
When I shall be a prince's mother-in-law.
[Knocking]
A visit at this time! Who's there?

[Enter **ONESTA**.

What now, my lady Faustine's maid?

ONESTA
The king has sent for you.

MARTHA
The king!

ONESTA
King

ALARDO
By the deceit of providence he has come back; and Guido has found out Faustine's escape. He commanded me to go and bring you, because he has heard about Eulalie; for Guido threatened me with flaying and pickling, and buttering and roasting. You are to come at once and meet the king and Guido and another lord at the tree in the gushet where the three roads meet, to go with them to the wood, where Eulalie and the prince, and Faustine and Cinthio are. If I would not tell him all, he would have minced me into collops, else he might have pulled my tongue out before I would have told. The king is going to pack you and Eulalie off this very night. 'The mad, old heifer,' says he, 'to set her low-bred cow to my royal bull.' And Cinthio is to be made into a ram—no, it was a ewe, Guido said: I think it was a ewe, though it struck me he meant an ox; and Faustine is to mew in a nunnery all her life.

MARTHA
The king come back, and Eulalie and I to be packed off to-night; Faustine, made a nun; you, to be roasted

ONESTA
Haste, haste. I'll tell you more as we go.

MARTHA
More! Save us! You have said more than enough.

[They go out.

ACT V

SCENE I.—An Open Space in the Wood

Enter **FELICE**, **BRUNO** and **TORELLO**.

FELICE
Do you remember what you must say?

TORELLO
I think so.
From Thessaly, that land of incantation,
Tetragrammaton,

Come Hecate and hear my supplication—

FELICE
Shemhamphorash.

TORELLO
Shemhamphorash.

FELICE
You must speak this word very loud; its virtue is great; and the greater mouth you give it, the stronger its power. Shout it again exultantly; for with this word properly spoken, a world might be created.

TORELLO
Shemhamphorash.

FELICE
Pronounced in a most redundant ore rotundo. No witch that ever culled simples with a brazen knife by moonlight could resist such a summons.

TORELLO
Will she indeed come forth to this?

FELICE
Like a cat from the water.

TORELLO
What shall I say then?

FELICE
The witch will question you and you must answer her.

TORELLO
What questions? Will she use a book? I could never learn catechism.

FELICE
Answer anything. It matters little what, so it be spoken reverently. This is the stone; place one foot on it; take off your hat; hold your sword high above your head; place your other hand upon your haunch: now, begin 'From Thessaly.'

TORELLO [Prompted by **FELICE**]
    From Thessaly, that land of incantation,
        Tetragrammaton.
    Come Hecate and hear my supplication,
        Shemhamphorash.
    On broomstick ride to grant what I shall ask,
        Tetragrammaton;
    Simple to thy skill will be the task,
        Shemhamphorash.

[Enter **SCIPIO** dressed like a witch.

SCIPIO
Thou comest to know if she whom thou lovest will be thine.
Swear by oak and ash and thorn to perform what rites I shall direct, and thou shalt know.

TORELLO
I swear.

SCIPIO
The oak is Jove's tree; thou hast sworn by Jove:
Mars' lances, Cupid's arrows are of ash;
To witness therefore hast thou summoned them:
The thorn is Mercury's; he binds thine oath.
Among the flags that, like a rushy curb
The streaming brook rein to an ambling pace,
With hands fast bound and eyes from light swathed close,
In upright patience shalt thou take thy stand.
If she thou lov'st loves thee, fate drives her here
Thy bondage to release, or rather change
To wedded slavery in rose-linked chains
That shackle willing lovers mutually.

TORELLO
What if she come not?

SCIPIO
Why, some other then,
Or man, or maiden will enfranchise thee.
If man, thy doom of single life is sealed;
If maid, in her behold a wife revealed.
Jove, Cupid, Mars, Mercury bless this rite;
Fail in the least, they curse thee from to-night.

[Goes out.

TORELLO
Need I do this? Stay! Gone—without a gift, too! An inhuman witch!
[Aside]
Am I mocked, I wonder? That can hardly be. I must go on: it were cowardly to be afraid. Yet would I watch these two.—Well, sirs, you heard the witch.

FELICE
It is a strange ceremony. Having sworn, you cannot evade it.

TORELLO
Tie my hands and bind my eyes.

FELICE
It is a most infallible test. I knew a knight who was scarce in the water before his mistress came and unbound him.

TORELLO
Do you laugh?

BRUNO
Who? I? No; I am as solemn as a hangman.

TORELLO
How deep is this stream?

FELICE
It cannot reach above your knees, being so shallowed by its width. Are you ready? Come along, then.

[Having pinioned and blind-folded **TORELLO** they lead him into the stream.—**CELIO** and **SYLVIA** enter, and pass into a grove.

 BRUNO [Aside]
Two mayers.

TORELLO
Is there any one coming?

FELICE
You must not speak. We will withdraw among the hazels. Let faith and courage console each other, and your spirit may have that comfort which your body lacks.

[Re-enter **SCIPIO.**

SCIPIO
How do you like the leeches' element? Have you made the acquaintance of any insinuating eels?

FELICE [Aside]
Hush! you must treat it solemnly. It is a dull nose that cannot scent hartshorn. He begins to sniff.

TORELLO
Leeches, eels! I pray you, how stand I for getting out should any evil thing attack me?

FELICE
Your back faces the only safe way; the stream is deeper before you than on your right; to the left the muddy bed would smother you; you stand on a stone. Cry on us if you are assailed.

TORELLO
I will. Go not far away.

FELICE
A speedy deliverance to you.

[**FELICE**, **BRUNO** and **SCIPIO** withdraw to the back of the stage.

TORELLO
Thanks.—Lord, lord, what love will make a man do! Here am I—Eulalie, when thou findest me thus thou wilt love me.

FELICE
Now, if we had a leash of hounds to loose on him, or a troop of charitable imps to pinch him for us.

[Enter **CINTHIO** and **FAUSTINE**.

BRUNO
More noctambulators.

FELICE
This is the prince's shepherd, and his sweetheart: if they observe Torello, they may help our plot.

CINTHIO
Bright-pinioned night now slacks her onward flight
And hovers towards its mid stage, to alight,
Furling her wings, one instant on the earth,
Ere emptying heaven for Aurora's birth,
That gladdens every morn. Here will we rest
Till night has sped a little further west.
O that we might recline between her wings,
And sail for aye her heavenly voyagings!

FAUSTINE
I would we might, but we must navigate
A vessel and an ocean less elate.
How far are we from thy Sebastian's boat?

CINTHIO
An hour will take us where it lies afloat.

FAUSTINE
Is this the forest's most secreted spot?

CINTHIO
Yes; none save shepherds visit it. Do not
Fear anything; and we will reach the shore
By pathways that are their peculiar lore.

[Enter **RUPERT** and **EULALIE**.

The prince and his beloved!

[**CINTHIO** and **FAUSTINE** conceal themselves.

RUPERT
Sit, Eulalie; this tree-trunk bids us rest.
Hush! hark! the nightingale, the lover's bird,
The throbbing pulse of night, panting its joy.
About this season he expects his mate,
And spends all day and night in rapturous toil
Upon a bridal-song to greet her with.
I think those twinkling midnight birds up there,
The stars, that seem to nestle in the leaves,
Utter such dulcet strains could we but hear.—
Now, tell me softly; did'st thou dream to-night?

EULALIE
Thou should'st have first inquired if I did sleep.
Whether I slept or not, I dreamt a dream,
The most entrancing and most lovable.

RUPERT
Did'st thou indeed! What was it all about?

EULALIE
I laid me on my bed, and couched the rose
That thou had'st given me in my bosom. Then
Its odour, packed with semblances of bliss,
Far-off delights, remembrances of songs,
And nameless sweets, all woven in a charm
Of strange awakening scent alone bestows,
Grew brightly visible; and in that halo
Sleep realised a shining rainbow crowd
Of gay unearthly beings, who, to notes
That never lark or nightingale imagined,
Tripped in the mazes of a wildering dance—
A poem in mute show.—Hark! some one comes.

[**RUPERT** and **EULALIE** retire.

[Re-enter Celio and **SYLVIA.** They seat themselves on the tree vacated by **RUPERT** and **EULALIE.**

TORELLO
Sweet voices! Methought I heard Eulalie's. O, come my love!
Shemhamphorash.

SYLVIA
Had any one save thee told me this tale

Discredit would have paid his waste of breath.
So dark that grove is, and its air so full
Of night's fantasticism, thy whispers low
May have been rounded to a meaning big
With sense that had no birth in thy intendment.
Did'st thou not tell me of a peopled star?
If there be such a jewel in the heavens,
Point out its light.

CELIO
That magnate brilliant,
Gleaming, opalesque, red, white, and blue,
Quivering and shuddering in its loveliness,
That star's inhabited.

SYLVIA
It is, indeed,
A bright, first-water sphere. And in it dwell
Oberon and Titania, and their elves.
Did'st thou say that?

CELIO
I said it, and it's true.

SYLVIA
King Oberon, a many years ago,
Divining that this grass-green, sea-green earth,
This emerald that sets off the golden sun,
Should be by mankind sadly under-priced;
That this fair hanging garden, swung for elves
And men to revel in, this glorious stage
In heaven's theatre, so gallantly
Hung out and decked for elves and men to grace,
This temple, wherein all might minister,
Should be o'er-rioted, abused, profaned;
That this globe, frescoed round by Nature's art,
Should lose its beauty in the sight of men—
Men's eyes being jaundiced by a golden lust
To prize much more the hills' bright excrement,
Than their elate and sun-gilt brows of strength;
That men, like children wearied of a toy,
Would spoil its loveliness, in pieces rending
To put it to some use, or ravish out
The useless secret of creation: he,
The fairy king, slow-winged and sad of heart,
Searched out a new home from the host of heaven,
And chose that star for him and his to dwell in.

CELIO
I said so.

SYLVIA
And, beside, that this strange science
Impart to thee a darling fairy did—
One of a company that roam the earth
To happy and inspire such clay-clad souls
As recognise their heavenly geniture,
And separate them from the loathly world:
And that this spirit visits earth to-night
To revelate some pleasure new to thee,
Which thou, sweetheart, art going to share with me?

CELIO
Hark to that singing! 'tis the fairy's voice.

RUPERT
We overheard you here unwillingly,
But with wills well inclined would now remain.

CELIO
That's as the fairy pleases. Here he comes.

CINTHIO [To **FAUSTINE**]
All are engrossed: no fear of our discovery.
We'll wait awhile, then slip unseen away.

FELICE [To **BRUNO**]
Here be miracles about to be.

[Enter **1st FAIRY**.

1st FAIRY
Song.
> On the mountain's crown,
> When the sun goes down,
> You may see me robed in the bright crimson.
> In the still mid-night
> When the moon shines bright,
> I shimmer down on a beam of light.
> I guide the mariner's crazy craft,
> When the billows are raging high.
> I glide before the wandering boor,
> And lead him safe to his own house door
> For love of charity.
> I hover near the poet's ear,
> And haunt him till he sings:

The minstrel's hand my unseen wand
Guides o'er the throbbing strings.
Whatever is joyful and makes the world glad,
That is my lot to do.
I never am weary, I never am sad,
For my work my play is too.

CELIO
He smiles; our number does not anger him.
List; he will tell us now unheard-of news.

TORELLO
Felice, Bruno! are you by?

FELICE
We are here. Whisper softly, or you may break the spell.

TORELLO
Who are those that talk and sing?

FELICE
I hear no talking and singing. The charm is acting: these voices which we cannot hear herald the approach of your deliverer.

TORELLO
I hope so; but perhaps it is my imagination. Have you really heard nothing? There were first several who spoke, and Eulalie's voice among them, and then an angel sang. O, that some one would come! It is horribly cold standing here.

BRUNO
Patience, patience.

SCIPIO
Patience, sir, is a great virtue.

TORELLO
But love is a greater; for were I not in love, I would have no patience.

1st FAIRY
The pleasance of our starry residence,
In human, bald speech inenarrable,
Transcends your dreams of Arcady and Eden.
Yet every year we all descend to earth,
Because our memories are steeped in joy,
Which was our ancient mundane element
When men were heroes and the world was young,
And life was laughter, love, and noble spleen:—
Alas, for you, poor actors! in Heaven's sight

Ye play an after-piece abjectly low!—
Also, because there are—how few they be!—
Who love true riches and despise the false,
We leave our unimagined paradise
Upon the first night that fair Pleiad, May,
Begins her soft ascendance o'er the year,
And bringing summer with us, visit earth.
Even now I see our elfin nation come,
Descending like a shower of frosty snow
For lightness, and for loveliness like Iris
Speeding in rainbow colours through night's gloom.
Look how the lightning or the light doth pass:
So have the fairies travelled from their star;
They left a minute since, and here they are.

[Enter **OBERON**, **TITANIA**, **PUCK**, and the **FAIRIES**. The **FAIRIES** dance and sing.

Song.
    Weave the dance and sing the song;
    Subterranean depths prolong
    The rainy patter of our feet;
    Heights of air are rendered sweet
    By our singing. Let us sing,
        Breathing softly, fairily,
        Swelling sweetly, airily,
    Till earth and sky our echo ring.
        Rustling leaves chime with our song;
        Fairy bells its close prolong,
            Ding-dong, ding-dong.
    Philomel, sing loud and high,
    Leader of our minstrelsy;
    No owl hoot, or raven cry;
    All glad sounds join harmony,
    And let no faintest discord sigh.
        Crickets chirrup merrily,
        And grasshoppers cheerily,
    Till our echo thrill the sky.
        Rustling leaves chime with our song:
        Fairy bells its close prolong,
            Ding-dong, ding-dong.

EULALIE
This is the harmony that filled my dream.

RUPERT
Perfumes of lilies, roses, violets—
Sweeter far than they: such a rich gust
Of warmth and scent they flood the air withal.

CELIO
That is Titania with the golden hair,
And wreath of moon-flowers pale, which shows, methinks,
Like lightning round the sun.

SYLVIA
And see, her robe!
It's a new colour. O, it aches my eyes!

RUPERT
And Oberon's a king, a very king.

EULALIE
My dream—this is my dream!

RUPERT
And to thy dream
I'll tell thee how I played god Morpheus.
But now with these good neighbours let us talk.

EULALIE
No; let us feast our eyes and then our ears.

TORELLO
More music and voices! This is no imagination: it is the charm's doing. I will say it again profounder.
Shemhamphorash.

RUPERT
Moonlight and madness! What a howl was that!

CELIO
What stands in the mid-stream?

SYLVIA
A man, bound, blinded.

EULALIE
It is Torello, sure.

RUPERT
And I see two
Who know full well how he comes in this plight.
What's Puck about?

[**PUCK** liberates **TORELLO**.

TORELLO

O hell! art thou the devil? Felice, Bruno, take this imp away. Ha! what sights are here? Angels, and fairies, and Eulalie and Rupert! Perdition! O perdition!

FELICE
Be calm. Who unbound you?

TORELLO
This little grinning demon.

FELICE
Where?

TORELLO
Here, on my shoulder. Do you not see him? And all this crowding crowd, and Rupert and Eulalie? Do you not? Do you not see them? Ah me! you cannot; for it is a vision. I will not suffer it. My doom is sealed. Farewell, fair Eulalie, farewell. Avaunt thou hairy fiend! Thou shalt not have me. O, you pinch me! Oh! oh!

[**TORELLO** runs out tormented by **PUCK**.

[**PUCK** re-enters shortly.

RUPERT
This is the wildest prank; we'll hear its source another time.

CELIO
Should not our queen of May interview the Fairies?

RUPERT
Well bethought.

EULALIE
Then I'll begin with thee. What elves are these,
Thou seem'st to lead in ordered companies?

2nd FAIRY
    That the fairy army is,
    Clad in rose-leaves, bravely worn;
    Pollen far outshines gold lace;
    Their helmets bright are husks of corn;
    Quivers of the adder's slough;
    Bows of legs of spiders slain;
    A cob-web string is strong enough
    For a spear-grass arrow's strain,
    With the sting of hornet tipped,
    In the dew of hemlock dipped.

EULALIE

And what are you, ye varied, restless ones?

3rd FAIRY

> We the fairies are who sleep,
> Blanketed and pillowed deep
> In the golden, blooming folds
> Of nightly-cradled marigolds.
> Some with evening's blushes meek
> Tinge the peach's downy cheek.
> Feathers stolen from butterflies
> Make our pencils: all the dyes
> Of all the flowers we fairies know
> How bright daffodils to gild
> In the saffron sunrise glow;
> To launder lilies in the snow;
> When midnight all the air has filled
> We dip in purple gloom the pansy;
> When Cupid over-rules our fancy
> For our loves we make incision;
> The daisies with our blood we dight,
> Loosened from its veined prison;
> When we haste upon our mission
> In a moonless, starless night,
> Fireflies, glow-worms lend us light.

EULALIE

Come hither, little brownie, dark and green.
I prithee, tell me what thy fellows bin.

4th FAIRY

> Wood-elves they, in russet dressed,
> And they love the lindens best.
> Hark, they hum our antique rune!
> A human fiddler learned the tune,
> And played it at a merry-making:
> Still he plays; the clowns still dance
> In a jolly, jigging trance;
> For them to rest there is no waking,
> Till that fiddler learn to play
> Backward our elfin melody.

EULALIE

And what are ye so beauteously dressed?

5th FAIRY

> River-spirits, golden-tressed,
> With blue eye, and light-blue vest.
> None can sing so sweet as we,

Joyfully or mournfully;
And our chant is ever ringing:
Such a spell is in our singing,
Every listener hears aright
His own thought from the water-sprite.

EULALIE
And ye?

6th FAIRY
We are sea-nymphs, sea-green-haired,
Liquid-voiced and liquid-eyed.
We will float with bosoms bared
On old Neptune's happy tide;
There our filmy smocks to bleach
In the sun, and soft west wind;
Mortals, gazing from the beach
Think them foam-crests, fairy-blind.

EULALIE
And ye, the fairiest of all the fairies?

7th FAIRY
We are most ethereal sprites,
Draped in merging rainbow lights.
Perfume is our dainty food;
Ever varying is our mood.
Sometimes in a rose we shine;
Now a girl's face make divine
For her sweetheart, lying hid
In her blush, or her eyelid:
Unfelt we swing upon a hair:
To be lovely's our sole care.

SYLVIA
Titania waves her wand. O, will she speak?

TITANIA
All manner of delight attend your loves:
That you are lovers tasks no intuition:
And we rejoice to think Cythera's son
His ancient craft plies with unbated skill,
Though there be some who hold he fled long since
For ever from his earthly hunting-ground,
While a usurper courses his preserves—
A hideous dwarf, disguised, who blindness feigns
And shoots forged bolts that are indeed of gold,
But cast in Hades, of no heavenly ore,

Lacking love's temper, and sweet-poisoned barb.
Truth has its part herein, sad sooth to tell;
For many a fight has Cupid with his foe,
And much the issue of their war is feared
In skyey quarters: well it is for you
That ye are lovers orthodox and true.
Every good wish is in this that I say—
May you be lovers till your dying day.
Wilt thou say something to them, Oberon?

OBERON
Bless you, fair lovers—benedicite.
Kind damsels, let me kiss you.

TITANIA
Nay—why, then,
If thou wilt kiss the maids, I'll kiss the men.

[They do accordingly.

OBERON
Mortals, farewell for ever and a day.
To-night we fairies wend the wide world round;
And this our visitation each new May
To summer sweetness mellows air and ground.
The winds kiss from our lips a perfumed spoil,
And store the pillaged wealth in woods and bowers;
Each fairy footstep swift impregns the soil,
And in our wake we leave a foam of flowers.
In orchard blossoms from our odoured hair
We shake rich drops that flavour all the fruit;
Nor lacks the grain our much-availing care!
Each thing is blessed where comes a fairy foot:
We bless all bridals true, all love that's chaste.—
Now, fairies, to the sea with utmost haste!

[**OBERON**, **TITANIA**, and the **FAIRIES** go out.

PUCK
Every trick that erst I played
    On horse or ox, on man or maid,
    On jealous husband, grandam old;
    On timid wight, or braggart bold,
    On lazy slut, or busy lass—
    To whom I through the keyhole pass,
    Pinching slattern black and blue,
    A tester dropping in thrift's shoe—
  To-night I merrily repeat,

And all sight and hearing cheat.
        Willy-wisp, spoorn, hag, or faun,
    Urchin, changeling, pixy, pan,
        All these shapes and names I bear,
        Pressing like a dread nightmare
        Full-fed losels, half-awake,
    Rustling like the fierce fire-drake,
        Shouting loud the whole night long
        Witching spell or laughing song.

VOICE
Come, come, come along!

PUCK
Hark! 'twas Oberon who cried
From the sandy wet seaside.

VOICE
Come, come, come away!

PUCK
I'll be with you, princely fay,
Ere again those words you say.

[Goes out.

EULALIE
Hush!

FELICE
This sport is o'er. We must go seek Torello.

[**FELICE**, **BRUNO**, and **SCIPIO** go out.

CINTHIO
Come, Faustine; this bright mask is played and done.
Fair pioneers, we'll follow you anon.

[**CINTHIO** and **FAUSTINE** go out.

[Enter **GREEN** and **IVY**, tipsy.

IVY
By the light of Hecate's lamp—lamp, lamp? What rhymes with lamp! Scamp? cramp?

GREEN
Damp.

IVY
Damp? Good.
>   By the light of Hecate's lamp,
>   May all poetry be damned;
>   And each stupid poet-scamp,
>   May his invention take the cramp!
There! that's genius!

SYLVIA
O Celio, come! I cannot bear these fools.

[**CELIO** and **SYLVIA** go out.

IVY
Here be people!

GREEN
And here be more!

[Enter **ALARDO**, **GUIDO**, **MARTHA**, **ONESTA**, and **MAYERS**, with **CINTHIO** and **FAUSTINE**, guarded.

EULALIE
Mother, what do you here?

MARTHA
You'll see anon.

ONESTA [To **FAUSTINE**] O, my lady, you must not blame me! I could not help it. My lord your father—

GUIDO
Peace, well-named hypocrite!
[Aside to **ALARDO**]
This is your son,
With that low maid on whom he would devolve
The varied riches of his royal blood.

ALARDO
Refer to his decree your daughter's case,
Thereby to see how far his judgment's warped.
[To **CONRAD**]
Reveal not yet your parentage, I pray.

RUPERT
Why, how now, Guido? Sir, what mean you thus
With all this mob to break upon us here?

GUIDO
My gracious prince, these two but now confessed—

What fear of torture from my daughter's maid
Had riven ours already—that to-night,
Faustine, having 'scaped by practices most vile,
Meant with this silly shepherd to elope,
He having stolen her heart from me, her sire;
Though by what means they interchanged their loves,
How spake, how saw each other, passes skill:
And both with fixed intent to rob your land
Of their two bodies and hidden wealth of issue,
In that same ship, whose captain is Sebastian
(Riders we have despatched to fetch him here),
Purposed themselves to carry off—fine caskets
Of so high value and unpriced contents,
All to your grace, and all to Belmarie,
And a fair moiety to me, belonging.
This knowing, and that, until time should serve
They here did hide, thinking the wood more safe
Than our exposed and pirate-haunted shores,
I, with these lords, came hither. On the way
We trained along with us these unbid Mayers,
Who must excuse themselves if they offend;
Though for their help in finding out this haunt,
Subserving thus the law, they might be shrived.
A strange and most sweet music led us on;
And we supposed to find the minstrels here,
And know from them of those love-guided truants.
In perpetration of their triple crime
We caught our night-errant lovers. Upon them
Immediate justice I do here demand
In your name, mine, and in that of the land.

RUPERT
Which thou and it and they shall surely have.
Stand from the shade, ye social rebels. What!
My Cinthio! thou should'st have trusted me.—
This is the final doom that I decree.
Guido, take thou thy daughter in one hand,
Her lover in the other. Mother mine,
Here is my hand and here is Eulalie's.
Lord Guido, thou next best blood to the throne,
Surrender here into this shepherd's arms
Thy well-beloved and only daughter, Faustine.
Good Martha, of the very lowliest stock,
On me, King Rupert, thy sweet child bestow.
I now revoke my first decree, and take
That title, which is mine, to make this right;
For kings are higher than all laws but love.
Do as we bid, lord Guido; join their hands,

As Martha now unites my love's and mine.
Do it, I say; or else by Hymen's torch
I'll marry thee to Martha, and so make
Three marriages, by which a king becomes
A peasant's husband, and a subject's son;
Obtains a mother—a poor fisher's widow—
Who brings with her a lordly father-in-law,
A gentle sister, and a simple brother:
Thus I, a king, beget more new affection
Than love, which not incites this my election.

ALARDO
Rash boy, forbear.

RUPERT
My father!

ALARDO
Yes, Rupert.
No ghost, in health, and likely long to live.
Leave go her hand; and you, girl, let his go.
Woman, be you more careful of your child.
We wait to be obeyed.

RUPERT
I'll not obey:
I owe no duty, know no king, but love.

EULALIE
Farewell, dear Rupert. Rupert and farewell
I say now finally: yet kiss me once.
My dream dispels before your father's frown:
Those fairies which we saw we did not see;
I am still half asleep: when I awake
My cheated eyes will weep their own deceit,
Viewing my chamber's walls so falsely real.
Go to your father, prince; I'll to my mother.

FAUSTINE
I have no father, and I have no king
Save thee, my Cinthio, and my dearest love.
I see her heart is almost split in twain;
But if they rive my body from thine arms,
My heart entire will stay there: I shall die.

ALARDO
I had forgot: you two need not to part;
Conrad will speak the barrier away.

CINTHIO
I do remember now two soothsayers.

RUPERT
I see them in my father and this lord.

CONRAD
You see aright. Shepherd, thou art my son.
I here have watched thee with a lynx's eyes,
And noted every motion of thy limbs,
Thy heart's each flutter and thy tongue's each word,
And every act; and in thy very sighs,
Thine eye's upturning, there is limned past doubt
A faithful copy of thy heaven-homed mother.
But let me see the chain that's round thy neck.
Thou art my son!

CINTHIO
My father!

GUIDO
Go, Faustine,
Go to him. Royal sir, my word is proved,
That women are but governed by their bloods.

ALARDO
And dogs, and men, and angels I presume.—
But what to do with my sad son I know not.

MARTHA
I'm going to disown thee, Eulalie.
Please it your gracious highness and fair prince,
This gentle lady is no child of mine.
Her parents both were noble: how they died,
And she, an infant, of her heritage
Was cozened by an uncle, I'll make plain
By names, dates, papers, birth-marks, jewellery.
I reared her as my own in low content,
And meant not to destroy her happiness
By telling her of her nobility,
Till she might claim her land with power to take.

ALARDO
Prove what thou sayest, and they may wed to-morrow.

RUPERT
Thanks, gracious father. It is true, I know.

What, Eulalie! hast thou no energy?
Art thou struck dumb? Wilt thou not spring to me?
How! Would'st thou have me woo thee o'er again?
A high delight! Then high-born maid, be coy.

EULALIE
O no, I need no wooing; but I fear
Thou'lt love me in a manner different.
A lady I would be to marry thee;
But with thy former love, pray love me still.

RUPERT
With that, and every kind of love, I will.
Thou art—O what thou art I cannot say!
I love thee, nor can tell how lovingly.

IVY
I'll make a ballad of this, a proper ballad—a ballad that would draw tears from a frog in the heart of a rock. By Hecate, I will!

[Enter **OFFICERS** with **SEBASTIAN.**

OFFICER
This is the captain we were sent to take.

ALARDO
Canst thou say aught by way of an excuse?

SEBASTIAN
King, I behold such happy faces here,
Glowing like stars in the grey morning air,
That I have little fear to say, I cannot.
It seems indeed that every star of heaven
With most auspicious aspect earthward turns.
I bring such tidings as will raise your brows
Much more than this new amity I see
Constrains surprise in me. Your appetites
Shall, when they have fed full of wonderment,
Fall to a second feast of happiness,
Admiring, welcoming and hearing told
The ships, their crews, and unconceived escapes.

ALARDO
What ships, crews, 'scapes?

SEBASTIAN
Those galleys four, ornate,
With all the gallant, living human freight

That sailed forth in the five, with wealth untold
Of bullion, spices, silks, and rarities,
Gathered in many lands and many seas,
Are in the harbour safe arrived but now.

ALARDO
I cannot speak. Kind Heaven, my knees I bow.

MAYERS
Long live the King! Long live Prince Rupert! Long live our May-Queen!

GREEN
Let us to the shore.

IVY
Ay, that's the word! Come, lads and lasses! There shall we have sight of ships we thought never to see, and shake hands that we thought death had shaken, and hear voices that we thought were singing with mermaids. O, there will be kissing and embarrassment, and sobbing and lacrimony! I will end my ballad with it.

CINTHIO
Sebastian, all our voyaging is past.

SEBASTIAN
And paradise attained at home at last.

IVY
Good captain, lead us on.

SEBASTIAN
I pray you, wait.

IVY
Sir, we have waited a year and a month, and can tarry no longer.
Come.

MAYERS
Away, away!

[**GREEN**, **IVY**, **SEBASTIAN**, and **MAYERS** go out.

ALARDO
Behold, the blinking dawn with sleepy eyes
Peers from her cloudy lattice in the skies,
Early astir to see if it be time
For Phoebus to awake and make day's prime.
Be glorious in thy rising, day-god bright,
For thou wilt usher us to that delight

We hardly dared to pray for: mark this day
With thy most splendid, most benignant ray;
For fate has blessed it, and time seems to make
A new departure—yea of life to take
A fresh lease: so, henceforth, our years shall date.—
Follow us lovers linked in hands and hearts
Like true love-knots that strength or skill ne'er starts.

[**ALARDO**, **CONRAD**, and **GUIDO** go out.

MARTHA
Eulalie!

EULALIE
Dear mother!

RUPERT
And mine too.

CINTHIO
Now, let us wash our faces in the dew.

RUPERT
O, I forgot th' observance of the day.
All hail my mistress and my Queen of May!

EULALIE
I am afraid that all our joys but seem,
And I shall yet awake out of a dream.

RUPERT
Have no such fear, my love.—Behold us, then,
Two happy maidens and two happy men.
Lo, wakened by the lark, his bellman true,
Armed with a torch that merrily doth shine,
Arrayed in saffron of the deepest hue,
The sun, like Hymen, comes with smile benign!
As long as his resplendent light shall burn,
May our love-tides increase, but never turn.

John Davidson – A Short Biography

John Davidson was born at Barrhead, East Renfrewshire on 11th April 1857, the son of Alexander Davidson, an Evangelical Union minister and Helen née Crocket of Elgin.

In 1862 the family moved to Greenock and Davidson began his education at Highlanders' Academy. From there he began his career, aged a mere 13, at the chemical laboratory of Walker's Sugarhouse refinery. A year later he returned to Highlander's, this time as a pupil teacher.

During his later employment at the Public Analysts' Office, 1870–71 he developed a keen interest in science which later became an important characteristic of his poetry. He returned once again to the Highlander's Academy, this time for four years, in 1872, again as a pupil teacher. In 1876 he spent a year at Edinburgh University before his first scholastic employment at Alexander's Charity, Glasgow which led to short periods of employment at various other schools over the following half a dozen years.

This led to a stint at Morrison's Academy in Crieff (1885–88), and in a private school at Greenock (1888–89).

In 1885 Davidson married Margaret McArthur and the marriage produced two children, Alexander (born in 1887) and Menzies (born in 1889).

Davidson's first published work was 'Bruce, A Chronicle Play', written in the Elizabethan style, and published by a local Glasgow imprint in 1886. Four other plays quickly followed; 'Smith, A Tragic Farce' (1888), 'An Unhistorical Pastoral' (1889), 'A Romantic Farce' (1889), and then the somewhat brilliant pantomime 'Scaramouch in Naxos' (1889).

By now he was very much immersed in literature and, in 1889, he ventured to London where he frequented the famous Fleet Street pub 'Ye Olde Cheshire Cheese' and joined the 'Rhymers' Club', a poets group that was based there.

Davidson was a prolific and hard-working writer. As well as his plays he wrote for the Speaker, the Glasgow Herald, and several other papers. He also wrote and had published several novels and tales, with perhaps the best being 'Perfervid' (1890).

With his reputation gradually providing an income he was also able to explore his true medium; Verse. 'In a Music Hall and Other Poems' (1891) together with 'Fleet Street Eclogues' (1893) were ample proof that he possessed a quite rare, genuine and distinctive poetic gift. Praise came from his peers including George Gissing and WB Yeats who wrote that it was: 'An example of a new writer seeking out new subject matter, new emotions'.

Davidson now turned further and further towards verse. In 1894 he published his most popular volume, 'Ballads and Songs' (1894), and this was followed by a further 'Fleet Street Eclogues' (Second Series) (1896) and by 'New Ballads' (1897) and 'The Last Ballad' (1899).

Davidson was a prolific writer. Besides the works cited, he wrote many other works including, 'The Wonderful Mission of Earl Lavender' (1895), a novel which extends his literary canon to flagellation erotica. He also contributed an introduction to Shakespeare's Sonnets (Renaissance edition, 1908), which, like his various prefaces and essays, shows him to be a subtle literary critic.

As the new century dawned Davidson was hard at work on a series of 'Testaments', in which he gave definite expression to his philosophy and these were published over a seven year period; 'The Testament of a Vivisector' (1901), 'The Testament of a Man Forbid' (1901), 'The Testament of an Empire Builder' (1902), and 'The Testament of John Davidson' (1908).

Though he played down any thought of himself as a philosopher, he expounded an original philosophy which was at once materialistic and aristocratic.

His later verse, which is often fine rhetoric rather than poetry, expressed his belief which is summed up in the last words that he wrote, "Men are the universe become conscious; the simplest man should consider himself too great to be called after any name." Davidson professed to reject all existing philosophies, including that of Nietzsche, as inadequate. The poet planned to expand and expound on his revolutionary creed in a trilogy entitled 'God and Mammon'. Only two plays, however, were written, 'The Triumph of Mammon' (1907) and 'Mammon and his Message' (1908).

In addition to his own work Davidson was a noted translator of other works which included Montesquieu's 'Lettres Persanes' (1892), François Coppée's 'Pour la Couronne' in 1896 and Victor Hugo's 'Ruy Blas' in 1904, the former being produced as, 'For the Crown', at the Lyceum Theatre in 1896, the latter as 'A Queen's Romance' at the Imperial Theatre.

Frank Harris, a member of the Rhymers' Club and himself a writer of erotic literature described him in 1889 as: "... a little below middle height, but strongly built with square shoulders and remarkably fine face and head; the features were almost classically regular, the eyes dark brown and large, the forehead high, the hair and moustache black. His manners were perfectly frank and natural; he met everyone in the same unaffected kindly human way; I never saw a trace in him of snobbishness or incivility. Possibly a great man, I said to myself, certainly a man of genius, for simplicity of manner alone is in England almost a proof of extraordinary endowment."

In 1906 he was awarded a civil list pension of £100 per annum and George Bernard Shaw did what he could to help him financially. However other issues were also circling besides poverty. Ill-health, and his declining intellectual powers, amplified by the onset of cancer, caused profound hopelessness and clinical depression.

Late in 1908, Davidson left London to live in Penzance in Cornwall. On 23rd March 1909, he left his house and was not seen again. There seemed no sound reason not to believe that he had done so with the intention of drowning himself. On an examination of his office a new manuscript was found. It was a poetry book; 'Fleet Street Poems', with a letter bleakly stating confirming, "This will be my last book."

Indeed in his philosophic book 'The Testament of John Davidson', published the year before his death, he anticipates this fate:

"None should outlive his power. . . . Who kills
Himself subdues the conqueror of kings;
Exempt from death is he who takes his life;
My time has come."

Davidson's body was not discovered until 18th September in Mount's cave by some fishermen. In accordance with his will it was now buried at sea. Strangely it seemed Davidson's wish that none of his unpublished works, nor any biography be published and "no word except of my writing is ever to appear in any book of mine as long as the copyright endures."

Davidson's poetry was a key early influence on important Modernist poets, in particular, his compatriot Hugh MacDiarmid, Wallace Stevens and T.S. Eliot.

John Davidson – A Concise Bibliography

The North Wall (1885)
Diabolus Amans (1885) Verse drama
Bruce (1886) A drama in five acts
Smith (1888) A tragedy
An Unhistorical Pastoral, A Romantic Farce (1889)
Scaramouch in Naxos (1889)
Perfervid: The Career of Ninian Jamieson (1890) with 23 Original Illustrations by Harry Furniss
The Great Men, And a Practical Novelist (1891) Illustrated by E. J. Ellis.
In a Music Hall, and other Poems (1891)
Laura Ruthven's Widowhood (with C. J. Wills) (1892)
Fleet Street Eclogues (1893)
The Knight of the Maypole, (1903)
Sentences and Paragraphs (1893)
Ballads and Songs (1894)
Baptist Lake (1894)
A Random Itinerary (1894)
A Full and True Account of the Wonderful Mission of Earl Lavender (1895)
St. George's Day (1895)
Fleet Street Eclogues (Second Series) (1896)
Miss Armstrong's and Other Circumstances (1896)
The Pilgrimage of Strongsoul and Other Stories (1896)
New Ballads (1897)
Godfrida, a play (1898)
The Last Ballad (1899)
Self's the Man, A tragi-comedy (1901)
The Testament of a Man Forbid (1901)
The Testament of a Vivisector (1901)
The Testament of an Empire Builder (1902)
A Rosary (1903)
The Knight of the Maypole: A Comedy in Four Acts (1903)
The Testament of a Prime Minister (1904)
The Ballad of a Nun (1905)
The Theatrocrat: A Tragic Play of Church and State (1905)
Holiday and other poems, with a note on poetry (1906)
The Triumph of Mammon (1907)
Mammon and His Message (1908)
The Testament of John Davidson (1908)
Fleet Street and other Poems (1909)

He was also a contributor to 'The Yellow Book' periodical

www.ingramcontent.com/pod-product-compliance
Lightning Source LLC
Chambersburg PA
CBHW021939040426
42448CB00008B/1148